D0707741

PRAYING
WITH PAUL

A Year of Daily Prayers
and Reflections
on the Words and Actions
of Paul

Eugene H. Peterson

HarperSanFrancisco
An Imprint of HarperCollins*Publishers*

PRAYING WITH PAUL. *A Year of Daily Prayers and Reflections on the Words and Actions of Paul.* Copyright © 1995 by Eugene H. Peterson. All rights reserved. Printed in the United States of America. No part of this book may be used or reproduced in any manner whatsoever without written permission except in the case of brief quotations embodied in critical articles and reviews. For information address HarperCollins Publishers, 10 East 53rd Street, New York, NY 10022.

HarperCollins®, 📖®, and HarperSanFrancisco™ are trademarks of HarperCollins Publishers Inc.

FIRST EDITION

Library of Congress Cataloging-in-Publication Data
Peterson, Eugene H.
    Praying with Paul : a year of daily prayers and reflections on
the words and actions of Paul / Eugene H. Peterson.
        p.   cm.
    ISBN 0–06–066433–9 (pbk.)
    1. Paul, the Apostle, Saint—Prayer-books and devotions—
English.   2. Bible.   N.T.   Epistles of Paul—Devotional
literature.   3. Devotional calendars.   I. Title.
BS2506.5.P47   1995   95–9275
242'.2—dc20   CIP

    95 96 97 98 99 ❖ BANWI 10 9 8 7 6 5 4 3 2 1

For Jane and Vincent Stubbs
a lifetime of Christian witness in Japan

Introduction

S T. PAUL, one of the earliest converts to the Christian faith, is the first to write what he experienced and believed. At least he is the first Christian writer whose writings survived so that we can now read them. (The Gospels, in the form we have them, were all written a little later.) Paul wrote letters, letters to Christian communities and friends, letters recognized early on by their readers as more than letters between friends. Christians heard the voice of God in these writings and lost no time in setting them apart as the Word of God, inspired by the Holy Spirit. We Christians have been reading them that way ever since, reading them as the authoritative Word of God. After the early church completed the task of gathering and authorizing as Holy Scripture the documents that we now designate the New Testament, Paul turned out to have contributed nearly a third of the pages, more than any other single person.

Paul's major presence as a writer of scripture is more than matched by his influence as a pray-er of scripture. In an arresting imperative, he once urged us to "pray all the time" (1 Thessalonians 5:17). We ask, usually in some astonishment, "And how in the world do you suggest we go about doing *that?*" The answer is no farther away than in the sentences that are right before our eyes: Paul writing is at one and the same time Paul praying. There is hardly a phrase on these pages that does not exhibit the personal intensity and devout attentiveness of a person simultaneously listening and responding to God. Sometimes the praying is exuberantly explicit—"All praise to the God and Father of our Master, Jesus the Messiah! Father of all mercy! God of all healing counsel!" (2 Corinthians 1:3); more often it is implicit—"Here's what I want you to do, God helping you: Take your everyday, ordinary life—your sleeping, eating, going-to-work and walking-around life—and place it before God as an offering" (Romans 12:1). Always the scripture and the prayer are fused. As Paul wrote, God the Holy Spirit was using Paul's words to create Holy Scripture; as he wrote, Paul was praying in the Spirit his obedience and faith and gratitude.

Scripture and prayer belong together. It is only in combination that they conceive Christ in us, form and shape life in the Spirit in us. In acquiring facility in bringing and keeping them together, we can hardly do better than spend a year with St. Paul, reading and praying what he wrote and prayed.

Scripture apart from prayer becomes bookish, pedantic, wooden, and brittle. Unprayed scripture atrophies to mere ink on paper. The once living and powerful Word of God, "sharp as a surgeon's scalpel" (Hebrews 4:12), if read and studied under the dominating authority of lexicon and grammar, soon becomes nothing more than a blunt-edged weapon of dogma. The God-breathed sacred writings "showing us truth, exposing our rebellion, correcting our mistakes, training us to live God's way" (2 Timothy 3:15–16), if used as a resource for theological systems and self-help programs, quickly devolve into a religious shopping mall where consumers randomly pick and choose whatever suits them.

Likewise, prayer apart from scripture ends up as bluster and bombast among some; among others, as wistful longing—what a person once described to me as "wishing upwards." Unscriptured prayer soon finds itself in a swamp of subjectivity—all ego and emotion; or in a sterile laboratory of technology—all formula and method. We hear rumors that prayer is power and so, lusting after power, we embrace prayer as a surefire way to make our mark in the world. Or we catch sight of a bumper sticker, "Prayer Changes Things," and knowing that we could sure use a change, give it a try—until we are distracted by the next bumper sticker. Scripture and prayer are not separate items in the Christian life; each occurs in the presence of the other—

scripture and prayer are partners. The Christian life is conducted as a living conversation between God and believer. God does not simply order us about; nor do we order God about. We converse. God speaks in command and invitation and blessing (scripture); we answer in obedience and faith and gratitude (prayer).

Since I was not able to use all of Paul's writings, I chose the five letters that provide the best range in both content and tone of Paul's remarkable writing-praying life: *Romans, 1 and 2 Corinthians, Colossians,* and *Philemon.* By arranging comments and reflection and prayer over 365 days, I hope to make Paul as accessible to my friends in the twentieth century as he was to his in the first century. I hope also that these daily readings and prayers will become a means for drawing my friends into conversation and prayer with one another, building and developing communities, whether small or large, of scripture-listening and prayer-answering followers of Jesus Christ.

Praying with Paul

JANUARY 1

"Passing It On to Others"
Read Romans 1:1–6

> Through him we received both the gener-
> ous gift of his life and the urgent task of
> passing it on to others who receive it by
> entering into obedient trust in Jesus.
>
> *Romans 1:5*

Paul's authority and qualifications come from God.
Academic or professional credentials are beside the
point in this work. Paul, introducing himself to the
Romans, identifies himself not in terms of what *he*
has done but in terms of what *God* has done.

How do you introduce yourself?

PRAYER: What a gift Paul's ministry has been in the
lives of your people, O God! Use his teaching and
preaching in my life, so that I will learn your truth
and be trained in your ways. *Amen.*

JANUARY 2

"I Greet You Now"

Read Romans 1:7

You are who you are through this gift and
call of Jesus Christ! And I greet you now
with all the generosity of God our Father
and our Master Jesus, the Messiah.

Romans 1:7

Rome, proud and famous, was the most important
city in the world. But, though no one knew it at the
time, it was already on its way to collapse. Meanwhile, within the city, there was a small community of Christians, obscure and beleaguered, who
were on their way to triumph.

How do you fit into the community you live in?

PRAYER: Lord God, I want to understand the place
where I live not primarily in terms of its monu-
ments and traditions, or its scenery and industry,
but as the place where your people live, the place
where your will is coming into being. *Amen.*

JANUARY 3

"Grace . . . and Peace"

Read Romans 1:7b

Grace to you and peace from God our
Father and the Lord Jesus Christ.

Romans 1:7b

Grace designates all God's action toward us as free
and good. *Peace* designates all the Spirit's work in
us as whole and healthy. The two words are Paul's
favorites in greeting his friends.

How do you greet people?

PRAYER: For your grace, great God, the generous
and creative will that redeems me, I praise you;
for your peace, the sure and certain blessings of
your salvation, I give you thanks. *Amen.*

JANUARY 4

"That's First"

Read Romans 1:8

I thank God through Jesus for every one of
you. That's first. People everywhere keep
telling me about your lives of faith, and
every time I hear them, I thank him.

Romans 1:8

The first item on Paul's agenda is thanksgiving.
The Roman Christians were not primarily problems to be solved but people to be appreciated. He
has other concerns that he will get to, but thanksgiving tops the list.

What is your primary attitude to others?

PRAYER: Increase, dear Lord, my capacity for appreciation. I want to look at my friends and see
signs of your creation. I want to observe my family and discern the workings of your love. I want
to listen to my neighbors and hear you speaking
through them to me, through Jesus Christ. *Amen.*

JANUARY 5

"I *Ask* Him to Clear the Way"
Read Romans 1:9–10

I ask him to clear the way for me to come
and see you.

Romans 1:10

We live in a tension between our desire and God's will. Paul believes that the two realities can converge. Meanwhile, he does not look for a simple solution by denying his desire on the one hand, or avoiding God's will on the other.

What desire of yours has gotten disconnected from God's will?

PRAYER: Transform, O Father, my needs into energies that will take the shape of obedience. Make my desires into prayers that will complete your salvation in others. I set your will at the center of my life, for Jesus' sake, and in his name. *Amen.*

"You Have *As* Much to Give Me"
Read Romans 1:11–12

But don't think I'm not expecting to get
   something out of this, too! You have as
   much to give me as I do to you.

Romans 1:12

Ministry is an *exchange* of gifts. It is always reciprocal and never the patronizing gesture of a superior giving to an inferior. None of us is so richly endowed that we need not receive; none so impoverished that we may not give.

What have you received from those to whom you have given?

PRAYER: Help me, God, to be equally good at blessing others and receiving blessings from them. Prepare my heart to receive gifts from those I had supposed had nothing to give. *Amen.*

"I Am a Debtor"

Read Romans 1:13–15

Everyone I meet—it matters little
  whether they're mannered or rude,
  smart or simple—deepens my sense
  of interdependence and obligation.

Romans 1:14

Before Paul begins his work of ministry, he ac-
knowledges his position as debtor. First he re-
ceives, then he gives. And there is no one from
whom he has not received. All his preaching,
then, is in the form of a thank-you note, a word
of appreciation for gifts received.

From whom have you received?

PRAYER: Give me the honesty and humility, dear
God, to see myself as debtor in one way or another to everyone I meet, and then the generosity
to say thank you, in the name and for the sake of
Jesus Christ. *Amen.*

"I'm Most Proud"

Read Romans 1:16

It's news I'm most proud to proclaim, this
    extraordinary Message of God's powerful
    plan to rescue everyone who trusts him,
    starting with Jews and then right on to
    everyone else!

Romans 1:16

For the person who knows, even sketchily, who
God is and the way he works, there can be nothing but boldness. But if we are more concerned
with what people think than with what God does,
it is possible to be ashamed rather than proud of
the gospel.

Have you ever been ashamed of the name of
Christ?

PRAYER: God in Christ, the more I learn of your
ways, the more sure I am of your victory; the
more I understand your grace, the more confident
I am of your power; the more I realize your righteousness, the more I want to live by faith. *Amen.*

"Shows Up in the Acts of Faith"
Read Romans 1:17

God's way of putting people right shows
up in the acts of faith, confirming what
Scripture has said all along: "The person
in right standing before God by trusting
him really lives."

Romans 1:17

The word "faith" describes God's way of being in
relationship to us; it also designates our way of
living in obedient trust with him. Faith is the
medium of gospel, the stuff of both God's revelation and our response.

What scripture does Paul quote?

PRAYER: Faithful God, increase my faith. Even as
you faithfully give yourself to me, revealing love
and establishing salvation, so give me faith to
continue in a long discipleship of rejoicing trust
in you. *Amen.*

"God's Angry Displeasure"

Read Romans 1:18

But God's angry displeasure erupts as acts
of human mistrust and wrongdoing and
lying accumulate, as people try to put a
shroud over truth.

Romans 1:18

God exposes falsehood so that truth can be recognized. He tears out the wrong so that the good can grow. God's wrath is not a wild and indiscriminate rage, but a focused concern.

How do you feel about God's anger?

PRAYER: Declare your truth, God, so that I may live cleanly in the bright light of your revelation in Christ. I do not want to live by the deceits of self-righteousness, or behind the pretenses of disguised wickedness. Even though it pains me, show me your righteousness. *Amen.*

JANUARY 11

"Neither Sense nor Direction"
Read Romans 1:19–23

People knew God perfectly well, but when
they didn't treat him like God, refusing
to worship him, they trivialized themselves into silliness and confusion so that
there was neither sense nor direction left
in their lives.

Romans 1:21

In the practice of idolatry, however sophisticated
and refined, thinking becomes crabbed and emotions are strangled by fantasies. True worship of
God floods us with truth's light so that our imaginations become splendid in adoration.

What does all creation proclaim?

PRAYER: Glorious Creator, I stand in awe in the
midst of these wonders: animals and flowers,
birds and trees, stars and mountains. Do not let
me be distracted by any of them from my love for
you, but use each as a way to deeper praise, to a
holier adoration. Amen.

"Traded the True God"
Read Romans 1:24–25

And all this because they traded the true
God for a fake god, and worshiped the
god they made instead of the God who
made them—the God we bless, the god
who blesses us. Oh, yes! Amen.

Romans 1:25

The exchange of the demanding truth of God for
easy lies about him has a most devastating result:
God lets us live out the results of our decision. Instead of climbing to the mountains of adoration,
we fall into the murky swamps of idolatry.

What is the worst punishment?

PRAYER: Precious Lord, surround me with guardian
protectors so that I may never be misled by the dis-
honorable lies of idolatry but always hold fast to the
truth of your lordship revealed in Jesus, in whose
name I pray. *Amen.*

"They Paid for It"
Read Romans 1:26–27

Sexually confused, they abused and defiled
    one another, women with women, men
    with men—all lust, no love. And then
    they paid for it, oh, how they paid for
    it—emptied of God and love, godless
    and loveless wretches.

Romans 1:27

The "big lie" is that sin brings pleasure. In fact, it leeches joy from our bodies and robs our spirits of vitality. The results are on display everywhere—bored and anemic sinners.

What natural penalties of sin have you experienced?

PRAYER: God, show me the adventures in virtue, the vitalities in righteousness, and the ecstasies of goodness so that I may pursue your ways undistracted by the lusts of the flesh and unaffected by the pride of life. *Amen.*

JANUARY 14

"Let Them Run Loose"

Read Romans 1:28–31

> Since they didn't bother to acknowledge
> God, God quit bothering them and let
> them run loose.

Romans 1:28

It is a most frightening prospect that people made in the image of God and created for the glory of God could be described as they are here. Remove God from the center of life and there is immediate and total collapse.

How many items are in Paul's list?

PRAYER: Merciful Christ, most of all I need your help in maintaining a fixed center to my life where your saving lordship is acknowledged. Grant that my eye may be single and my heart pure. *Amen.*

JANUARY 15

"They Hand Out Prizes"
Read Romans 1:32

They know perfectly well they're spitting in
God's face. And they don't care—worse,
they hand out prizes to those who do
the worst things best!

Romans 1:32

The devil's cheerleaders, provocatively dressed and
bursting with enthusiasm: they have ruined their
own lives and now applaud the ruination of others' lives. The coarse hand-clapping is a vulgar par-
ody of the praise that animates the heart of faith.

Compare this with 1 Corinthians 13:6.

PRAYER: God, defend me against the corrupting
approval of those who applaud my worst instincts
and flatter my pride. I resolutely turn my back on
them and care only for your "Well done." *Amen.*

JANUARY 16

"It Takes One to Know One"

Read Romans 2:1

> Those people are on a dark spiral down-
> ward. But if you think that leaves you
> on the high ground where you can point
> your finger at others, think again. Every
> time you criticize someone, you con-
> demn yourself. It takes one to know one.
>
> Romans 2:1

Knowledge of sin must not be used to label others, but only to scrutinize ourselves. Alexander Whyte, a great diagnostician of sin, responded to the news of the arrest of a prominent citizen in Edinburgh with a shuddered, "It might have been me!"

Is there any sin of which you are not capable?

PRAYER: God, you know how I love discovering the faults in others: how delighted I am when I detect a flaw in my neighbors. Convert my interest in sin from gossip to confession: search my heart and see if there be any wicked way in me. *Amen.*

JANUARY 17

"Or Did You Think?"

Read Romans 2:2–4

Or did you think that because he's such
a nice God, he'd let you off the hook?
Better think this one through from the
beginning. God is kind, but he's not soft.
In kindness he takes us firmly by the
hand and leads us into a radical life
change.

Romans 2:4

God, who has an eternal love for the sinner, has no
tolerance for the sin. The person who interprets
God's kindness as indulgence, misinterprets it.

Give a personal instance of presuming on
God's kindness.

PRAYER: Eternal God, how grateful I am for your
kindness, your endless forgiveness, your patient
disciplining of me. Let me never forget the pain
that my sin causes you or others, and use that
memory to deepen my repentance. *Amen.*

JANUARY 18

"If You Go Against the Grain"
Read Romans 2:5–8

If you go against the grain, you get splin-
ters, regardless of which neighborhood
you're from, what your parents taught
you, what schools you attended.

Romans 2:6

What we do has eternal consequences. Our
"works," whether our presumptuous refusal to
take seriously God's word or our repentant response to his grace, make a difference.

Compare this with Psalm 1.

PRAYER: Father, your word is plain and your way is
clear: I choose the path of life. Help me to be
steady in my decision and persevering in my faith,
and so receive the gift of eternal life in Jesus
Christ. Amen.

"He Makes Up His Own Mind"
Read Romans 2:9–11

God pays no attention to what others
say (or what you think) about you.
He makes up his own mind.

Romans 2:11

Life is not fair. We experience prejudices, discriminations, and inequities in every area of our existence. But there is one grand exception: God is
fair. In that which matters most and in that which
is the center, there is no partiality.

What discriminations have you experienced?

PRAYER: Gracious Lord, I come before you without caution and without fear. I do not presume
upon your mercy and I will not cower before
your judgments, for I know that in Christ you do
all things well. *Amen.*

"Takes into Account"
Read Romans 2:12–16

The Message from God that I proclaim
through Jesus Christ takes into account
all these differences.

Romans 2:16

Why do we waste words speculating on how God
will deal with those who live under conditions different from ours—the "good pagans," for instance,
and the "innocent" heathen? Is it not enough that
we are confident that God will be thorough and
just and merciful?

Compare this with John 21:22.

PRAYER: God, keep me from vain curiosity regarding the destiny of others. Prevent me from prying
into the secrets that are already known to you.
Help me to be faithful in my sphere of duty, trusting in your mercy and justice for me and for all
your creation. *Amen.*

JANUARY 21

"Who Is Going to Guide You?"
Read Romans 2:17–24

While you are guiding others, who is
going to guide you? I'm quite serious.
While preaching "Don't steal!" are you
going to rob people blind? Who would
suspect you?

Romans 2:21

Charles Dickens likened his Pecksniff to a "direction-post, which is always telling the way to a place and never goes there." It is easier to apply a truth to you than to me. It is far easier to show you the way than to travel it myself.

What do you tell others that you don't do yourself?

PRAYER: Lord Jesus, convert all the information I have of you into a personal relation with you, so that what I learn about you I will live, and what I apprehend about you I will experience. *Amen.*

JANUARY 22

"Not of a Knife on Your Skin"
Read Romans 2:25–29

Don't you see: It's not the cut of a knife
that makes a Jew. You become a Jew by
who you *are*. It's the mark of God on
your heart, not of a knife on your skin,
that makes a Jew. And recognition comes
from God, not legalistic critics.

Romans 2:29

Literal obedience is no substitute for spiritual relationship. A religious act maintains authenticity only when it continues to express a heart-rooted commitment to God. Otherwise, it is a fake, no matter how exactly and faithfully it is performed. Compare Matthew 23:16–26.

PRAYER: Keep my life, O Christ, authentic and personal. Cultivate my heart so that it will receive the seed of your word and grow good fruit. Weed out all that is dead and worthless. *Amen.*

"So What Difference Does It Make?"
Read Romans 3:1—4

So what difference does it make who's a
Jew and who isn't, who has been trained
in God's ways and who hasn't?

Romans 3:1

Everyone has a special place in God's work. The special place of the Jews did not mean that God loved them more (as some presume) nor that they were exempt from judgment (as some assumed). Their role was to be the historical focus for revelation.

What is your special place?

PRAYER: God, if I am not a prima donna neither am I a zero. I will find my place in your salvation by listening to your word and being diligent in my allotted task today. By your grace I will love and speak and act in the name of Jesus to the greater glory of God. Amen.

JANUARY 24

"A Most Emphatic No!"

Read Romans 3:5–8

But if our wrongdoing only underlines and
confirms God's right-doing, shouldn't
we be commended for helping out?
Since our bad words don't even make a
dent in his good words, isn't it wrong
of God to back us to the wall and hold
us to our word? These questions come
up. The answer to such questions is no,
a most emphatic No! How else would
things ever get straightened out if God
didn't do the straightening?

Romans 3:5–6

The question ("if our wrongdoing only underlines and confirms God's right-doing, shouldn't
we be commended for helping out?") is superfi-
cially logical and fundamentally silly. God wants
us whole, free from every enervating and death-
dealing sin. His faithfulness is a triumph over (not
a license for) our unfaithfulness.

Why is sin always wrong?

PRAYER: God, I try every dodge to avoid your
grace—arguments, excuses, sophistries—and you
steadily repeat your love and affirm my salvation.
Thank you for your persevering patience. Amen.

"We All Start Out as Sinners"
Read Romans 3:9–18

So where does that put us? Do we Jews
get a better break than the others?
Not really. Basically, all of us, whether
insiders or outsiders, start out in identical conditions, which is to say that
we all start out as sinners.

Romans 3:9

The moment we decide that there is nothing to hope for from goodness in ourselves, we are ready to receive everything from God. We learn the bad news, that we cannot be righteous by our own or others' efforts, and then discover the good news: our righteousness is in Christ.

What scriptures does Paul quote?

PRAYER: Help me, dear God, to honestly look at myself, without evasions, without defenses, and then when I see myself truly, not to despair but to hope in your great promises of salvation. *Amen.*

JANUARY 26

"The Same Sinking Boat"
Read Romans 3:19–20

> This makes it clear, doesn't it, that what-
> ever is written in these Scriptures is not
> what God says *about others* but *to us* to
> whom these Scriptures were addressed
> in the first place! And it's clear enough,
> isn't it, that we're sinners, every one of
> us, in the same sinking boat with
> everybody else?
>
> Romans 3:19

Imaginative as we are and inventive as we are, there is one thing we cannot make and that is righteousness. The law exposes the futility of trying to do on our own what can be done only by God working in us.

Why is God's law both welcome and unwelcome?

PRAYER: Christ, receive me in both my weakness and my strength; both my shame and my pride. Use what you find in me to make me what you will for me, a life of freedom in faith. *Amen.*

"The God-Setting-Things-Right"
Read Romans 3:21–22

> But in our time something new has been
> added. What Moses and the prophets
> witnessed to all those years has happened.
> The God-setting-things-right that we
> read about has become Jesus-setting-
> things-right for us.
>
> Romans 3:21

God makes things right. Righteousness is not
what we do to please God but what God does that
makes it possible for us to live in a pleasing relationship to him. We never get things right, but we
can participate by faith in what he does that is
right.

What is the difference between your righteousness and God's?

PRAYER: What I cannot make for myself, O God,
create in me: goodness and forgiveness, and peace.
I accept your redemption, and praise you for making me what I was not, in Jesus Christ. Amen.

"God Sacrificed Jesus"
Read Romans 3:23–26

God sacrificed Jesus on the altar of the
world to clear that world of sin. Having
faith in him sets us in the clear. God
decided on this course of action in full
view of the public—to set the world
in the clear with himself through the
sacrifice of Jesus, finally taking care of
the sins he had so patiently endured.

Romans 3:23–26

Being "set in the clear," accomplished in Jesus
Christ on the cross, is the exchange of our sin for
God's righteousness. Christ does for us what we
cannot do for ourselves and our lives are, miracu-
lously, acceptable to God.

What are some personal implications for you
being "set in the clear"?

PRAYER: Receive, Lord Jesus Christ, my thanksgiving: I am clean and new, alive and joyous. I am
alive by your act in a way I never could be on my
own. All thanks to your great name. *Amen.*

"By Letting Him"
Read Romans 3:27–28

Our lives get in step with God and all
others by letting him set the pace, not
by proudly or anxiously trying to run
the parade.

Romans 3:28

If the new life is a gift that I receive by faith, then
I can live in simple, honest, unassuming leisure,
while the unattractive arrogance of stuffy moral
rectitude simply disappears.

Why is it impossible to believe and boast at the
same time?

PRAYER: Keep me faithful, faithful God. Always
depending upon you, always trusting in your
goodness, ever hoping in your will as you affirm
and reveal it in Jesus Christ. *Amen.*

JANUARY 30

"One"

Read Romans 3:29–31

How could it be otherwise since there is
only one God? God sets right all who
welcome his action and enter into it,
both those who follow our religious
system and those who have never heard
of our religion.

Romans 3:30

We do not pay enough attention to the revolutionary realization that God is one: there is not
one plan for this group of people and another
plan (or no plan) for that group. There is a single,
well-coordinated plan for every person's salvation. Everything is attached to the center, and the
center is God.

What argument is Paul refuting?

PRAYER: Even as you are gathering all history together, Father, gather all the pieces of my life together and make a single flaming response to you,
in the name of Jesus and the power of your Spirit.
Amen.

"Abraham"

Read Romans 4:1–5

What we read in Scripture is, "Abraham
entered into what God was doing for
him, and that was the turning point.
He trusted God to set him right instead
of trying to be right on his own."

Romans 4:3

Faith is not an innovation of upstart Christians; it is the foundation established by the first Hebrew, Abraham. The principle of faith that characterizes the gospel is also basic to everything that the people of God had experienced for nearly two thousand years.

What was "the turning point" for Abraham?

PRAYER: Father, I thank you for deep roots, well watered and richly nourished in the fulfilled promises and completed lives of my ancestors in faith. *Amen.*

"David Confirms"

Read Romans 4:6–8

David confirms this way of looking at it,
saying that the one who trusts God to
do the putting-everything-right without
insisting on having a say in it is one
fortunate man.

Romans 4:6

After Abraham, David is the greatest of the ancestors. His testimony corroborates Abraham's—faith is the only way of being in relation to God. What is more, there is no authority that can be cited to the contrary.

How does Psalm 32 support the argument?

PRAYER: Keep me attentive, God, to what you say to me and indifferent to what others say about you. Deepen my knowledge and understanding of your word in scripture. *Amen.*

"Before He Was Marked by Circumcision"
Read Romans 4:9–12

> Abraham is also, of course, father of those
> who have undergone the religious rite
> of circumcision not just because of the
> ritual but because they were willing to
> live in the risky faith-embrace of God's
> action for them, the way Abraham lived
> long before he was marked by circum-
> cision.
>
> Romans 4:12

To insist on certain religious practices as entrance
requirements for being among God's people is
putting the cart before the horse. Religious practice, in this case circumcision, doesn't make anything happen; it is only a sign that something has
happened—by faith.

Why was circumcision important?

PRAYER: Father, I pray that none of the things I do
will get in the way of who you are, and who I am.
Help me to appreciate the usefulness of religious
practice but never let it substitute for the act of
faith. Amen.

FEBRUARY 3

"An Ironclad Contract"
Read Romans 4:13–15

If those who get what God gives them only
get it by doing everything they are told
to do and filling out all the right forms
properly signed, that eliminates personal
trust completely and turns the promise
into an ironclad contract.

Romans 4:14

God is personal and operates personally—that is,
by faith. To abstract him into a "contract" does violence to every part of scripture. The contract has
a function, but it is not to lead us to righteousness—it never did that and never can.

Read Genesis 17:4–8.

PRAYER: I want, Lord, to respond to you and not a
"truth" about you. Show me by your Spirit your
personal will under every law and contract and
your revealed mercy behind every tradition. *Amen.*

"Something Out of Nothing"
Read Romans 4:16–17

> Isn't that what we've always read in Scripture, God saying to Abraham, "I set you up as father of many peoples"? Abraham was first named "father" and then *became* a father because he dared to trust God to do what only God could do: raise the dead to life, with a word make something out of nothing.
>
> Romans 4:17

If the gospel were not by faith, through grace, God would be under our control and we would have, not a gospel, but just one more chapter in the long and corrupt story of humankind's effort to wield power.

What does it mean, "God made something out of Abraham when he was a nobody"?

PRAYER: Give me an understanding, Lord, quick to perceive your ways and a faith glad to accept them. Instead of trying to get you to do things my way, help me to understand the way you do things, through Jesus Christ. *Amen.*

"He Plunged into the Promise"
Read Romans 4:18–25

He didn't tiptoe around God's promise
asking cautiously skeptical questions.
He plunged into the promise and came
up strong, ready for God, sure that God
would make good on what he had said.
Romans 4:18

God mattered more to Abraham than evidence. Abraham is great, not because he was first to be circumcised, but because when all the evidence was on the other side, he believed in God.

What is your greatest test of hope?

PRAYER: I am far too concerned with so-called evidence, God. I examine, I weigh, I judge. All the while you are doing things that I never guessed could be done, creating relationships I did not know were possible. Help my unbelief. *Amen.*

"Set Us Right with Him"

Read Romans 5:1

By entering through faith into what God
has always wanted to do for us—set us
right with him, make us fit for him—we
have it all together with God because of
our Master Jesus.

Romans 5:1

Setting us right means that the central disturbance
of our lives is cleared up. When that happens, the
center of our life is poised and secure—at peace.
The great thing that God does for us is connected
with the great thing that we need.

What do you need?

PRAYER: Dear Lord, I thank you for setting things
right for me through Jesus Christ: do your daily
work now of arranging and rearranging all the
parts of my life so that they work in harmony with
your will. Amen.

FEBRUARY 7

"Open"

Read Romans 5:2

And that's not all: We throw open our
doors to God and discover at the same
moment that he has already thrown
open his door to us. We find ourselves
standing where we always hoped we
might stand—out in the open spaces of
God's grace and glory, standing tall and
shouting our praise.

Romans 5:2

How do we get through to God? How do we find
the opening that will let us into the realm of eternal
life? Everywhere and always in scripture the
answer is Jesus Christ, the door.

How does Jesus Christ open things up to God
for you?

PRAYER: You have opened wide the door, O God.
Help me now to walk through it, not delaying,
not detouring. I would no longer live at a distance
from you, but intimately in your presence, in love.
Amen.

FEBRUARY 8

"Even When"

Read Romans 5:3–5

> There's more to come: We continue to
> shout our praise even when we're
> hemmed in with troubles, because
> we know how troubles can develop
> passionate patience in us.
>
> Romans 5:3

Christian experience somersaults our attitudes toward suffering: we discover that it is productive, not wasting. No matter how unlikely it seems, the evidence is overwhelming: suffering is a link in a process that arrives at the glory of God.

Why does a Christian rejoice in suffering?

PRAYER: Father in heaven, when I fail to see your hand in unpleasant pain or inconvenient duty, restore the deep insight that comprehends your love working through everything. *Amen.*

"We Were of No Use"

Read Romans 5:6–8

But God put his love on the line for us by
offering his Son in sacrificial death while
we were of no use whatever to him.

Romans 5:8

The benefits of the death of Christ are not what
we earn by being good; they are something we
are given because we are incapable of being good.
Christ is not a reward; he is a rescue.

What does Christ's death mean for you?

PRAYER: You have done, O Christ, what no one
either would or could do. I live by your grace, and
by your love am what I could not be. Thank you
for your unprecedented, unimaginable love. *Amen.*

"Now That We're at Our Best"
Read Romans 5:9–11

If, when we were at our worst, we were
    put on friendly terms with God by the
    sacrificial death of his Son, now that
    we're at our best, just think of how our
    lives will expand and deepen by means
    of his resurrection life!

Romans 5:9

There is a double meaning in the phrase "on
friendly terms with God" ("saved"). It means to
be rescued from certain destruction; it also means
to be restored to an original and intended health.
The meanings together produce the conclusion,
rejoice!

What does friendship with God mean?

PRAYER: All praise to you, O Christ, for your life,
which saves me for joyful living. All praise to you,
dear Lord, for your death, which saves me from
destruction. Amen.

"Adam to Moses"
Read Romans 5:12–14

> So death, this huge abyss separating us
> from God, dominated the landscape
> from Adam to Moses. Even those who
> didn't sin precisely as Adam did by
> disobeying a specific command of God
> still had to experience this termination
> of life, this separation from God. But
> Adam, who got us into this, also points
> ahead to the One who will get us out
> of it.
>
> Romans 5:14

We are in a common predicament because of our common ancestor: we sin, and we die. Even if we sin in different ways than Adam, our death is the same. And so we need a common salvation.

What was Adam's sin? What is yours?

PRAYER: You, O God, understand my origin and my destiny, the tangled centuries of my ancestry and the bright promises of my eternity. Save me from my past in Adam and equip me for my future in Christ. *Amen.*

"Life-Giving Gift"

Read Romans 5:15–17

There's no comparison between that death-
dealing sin and this generous, life-giving
gift. The verdict on that one sin was the
death sentence; the verdict on the many
sins that followed was this wonderful
life sentence.

Romans 5:16

The logic of the gospel is symmetrical: just as one
man's sin involved us all in death, so one man's
gift makes us all alive. But if there is similarity in
the process, there is contrast in the results, for
death cannot be compared with life.

How is Jesus better than Adam?

PRAYER: Lord Jesus, I thank you for turning everything around for me. Everything is possible because you are at the one place to make all the difference. Amen.

"One Man Said Yes to God"
Read Romans 5:18–19

One man said no to God and put many
people in the wrong; one man said yes
to God and put many in the right.

Romans: 5:19

Until we grasp the hopeless condition to which
we are condemned we are not in a position to appreciate the wonder of Jesus Christ. But having re-
alized our condition, every detail we learn about
Jesus reveals another glorious aspect of our salvation.

What does "put many in the right" mean?

PRAYER: Dear God, your strategy for salvation is
simple yet profound. I can understand it perfectly,
and yet I can never understand it. Thank you for
starting right where I am and then taking me to
where you are. *Amen.*

"Grace . . . Invites Us into Life"
Read Romans 5:20–21

All sin can do is threaten us with death,
   and that's the end of it. Grace, because
   God is putting everything together again
   through the Messiah, invites us into life—
   a life that goes on and on and on, world
   without end.

Romans 5:21

We can never get the jump on God! The more active we are in sin, the more active he is in doing something about our sin. His solution always outclasses our problem.

How does "passing laws against sin" "produce more lawbreakers"?

PRAYER: "Amazing grace—how sweet the sound—That saved a wretch like me! I once was lost, but now am found, Was blind, but now I see" (John Newton, "Amazing Grace," *The Hymnbook*, 275). *Amen.*

FEBRUARY 15

"I Should Hope Not!"

Read Romans 6:1–2

So what do we do? Keep on sinning so God
can keep on forgiving? I should hope
not! If we've left the country where sin
is sovereign, how can we still live in our
old house there? Or didn't you realize
we packed up and left there for good?

Romans 6:1–2

Do we deliberately and repeatedly break our arms
because we are on friendly terms with a good or-
thopedic surgeon? No more do we deliberately
maim our spirits because we have a gracious Savior.
    Do you ever presume on grace?

PRAYER: God, you are far more imaginative in grace
than I am in sin. Your answers are always more
comprehensive than my questions. In gratitude I
live in joyful and obedient faith, by your grace.
Amen.

"Old Country . . . New Country"
Read Romans 6:3–4

When we went under the water, we left
the old country of sin behind; when we
came up out of the water, we entered
into the new country of grace—a new
life in a new land!

Romans 6:4

Descent into the water is a burial: we are dead to
our previous life of sin. Ascent from the water is a
resurrection: we are alive to eternal life.

What does your baptism mean to you?

PRAYER: As I recall the fact of my baptism, dear
Lord, deepen my faith in your death and resurrection at work in me. I do not want to squander
such a glorious heritage in careless indolence, but
live it to the full in faith. *Amen.*

"Our Old Way of Life"

Read Romans 6:5–9

Could it be any clearer? Our old way of life
was nailed to the Cross with Christ, a
decisive end to that sin-miserable life—
no longer at sin's every beck and call!

Romans 6:6

We know that sin is not limitless, that sin is not
the last word. The crucifixion of Christ exhausted
the power of sin. The Christian knows that no one
needs to continue living under sin's dominion.

What does Christ's crucifixion mean to you?

PRAYER: Free me, Christ, from the lies I have been
told about sin. Remove every trace of glamour
that lingers around it in my imagination so that I
can see it as it really is, a dead thing with no power
to give joy or purpose. *Amen.*

FEBRUARY 18

"The End of Death-as-the-End"
Read Romans 6:10–11

> We know that when Jesus was raised from the dead it was a signal of the end of death-as-the-end. Never again will death have the last word. When Jesus died, he took sin down with him, but alive he brings God down to us.
>
> Romans 6:10

Christ accomplished salvation completely. We don't have to redo any part of it. We can devote all our energy to matters of life without having to spend a single moment excusing or defending or atoning for the dead sins of the past.

How will you live today?

PRAYER: Lord Jesus Christ, I thank you that I don't have to spend any time today languishing in futile regret or busily proving my worth, but can throw myself into a life of joy and faith and love. *Amen.*

"Throw Yourselves"
Read Romans 6:12–14

> Throw yourselves wholeheartedly and full-
> time—remember, you've been raised
> from the dead!—into God's way of doing
> things.
>
> Romans 6:13

No act of sin is necessary; no wickedness is in-
evitable; no wrong is fated. Because of Christ's
death we are free to choose the right, to elect the
good, and to choose God.

What is the difference between tyranny and
freedom?

PRAYER: I present every part of my body and spirit
to your will, O God. Take all the parts of me that
you have so marvelously created and use them in
tasks of redemptive love, through Jesus Christ my
Lord. *Amen.*

"Offer Yourselves"

Read Romans 6:15–16

Offer yourselves to the ways of sin, for
instance, and it's your last free act. But
offer yourselves to the ways of God and
the freedom never quits. All your lives
you've let sin tell you what to do. But
thank God you've started listening to a
new master, one whose commands set
you free to live openly in his freedom!

Romans 6:16

Every act of obedience is a blow struck for freedom. In obedience to Christ our freedom develops and matures. In servitude to sin our freedom
atrophies and finally hardens into a fixed slavery.

Do you think of obedience as bondage or freedom?

PRAYER: Lord and Master, release me from the in-
hibitions of base impulse and the restrictions of
sinful habit. Command the acts that will lead me
into a free and open life of righteousness. *Amen.*

FEBRUARY 21

"Expansive in Holiness"
Read Romans 6:17–19

I'm using this freedom language because
it's easy to picture. You can readily
recall, can't you, how at one time the
more you did just what you felt like
doing—not caring about others, not
caring about God—the worse your life
became and the less freedom you had?
And how much different is it now as
you live in God's freedom, your lives
healed and expansive in holiness?

Romans 6:19

The Big Lie is that the more we do what we feel
like doing, the more we experience freedom. The
Big Truth is that once we start "listening to a new
master," the more we enter the vast wholeness and
immense freedom for which we were created.

What is holiness?

PRAYER: Dear God, you made me and know what
I am good for. In these next few hours, show me
just one part of my life—an attitude? an act?—that
I can offer to you and experience a deeper freedom. *Amen.*

"Where Did It Get You?"

Read Romans 6:20–23

As long as you did what you felt like doing,
    ignoring God, you didn't have to bother
    with right thinking or right living, or
    right *anything* for that matter. But do you
    call that a free life? What did you get
    out of it? Nothing you're proud of now.
    Where did it get you? A dead end.

Romans 6:21

The unbeliever is a most impractical person. For
what is more impractical than working hard all
your life and getting paid with nothing more than
an expensively framed death certificate?

What do you get out of being a Christian?

PRAYER: God, I put myself under your orders and
commit myself to your commands. In faith I receive your life eternal, and thankfully praise you
for your gifts in Jesus Christ. *Amen.*

"The Law"

Read Romans 7:1–3

You shouldn't have any trouble understanding this, friends, for you know all
the ins and outs of the law—how it
works and how its power touches only
the living.

Romans 7:1

The law—the term Paul uses to summarize the whole paraphernalia of religion—has a strictly limited usefulness. The gospel proclaims a reality that surpasses limits, setting forth a life of the spirit that is eternal.

Do you understand what Paul means by "the law"?

PRAYER: Lord Jesus, help me to see clearly the difference between law and gospel, between regulations made to manage sin and your resurrection, which creates eternal life. *Amen.*

"No Longer Shackled"

Read Romans 7:4—6

But now that we're no longer shackled
to that domineering mate of sin, and
out from under all those oppressive
regulations and fine print, we're free to
live a new life in the freedom of God.

Romans 7:6

The transition from law to gospel does not consist
of a disloyal repudiation of the old way followed
by fickle experimentation with the new. God himself discharges us from one way of life and commands us to another so that we "live a new life in
the freedom of God."

What do you owe to the law?

PRAYER: I want, dear Lord, to feel in my bones and
understand in my heart the ways of the Spirit. Let
your truth penetrate deep with me, for Jesus' sake.
Amen.

"Clear Guidelines"

Read Romans 7:7–8

But I can hear you say, "If the law code was
   as bad as all that, it's no better than sin
   itself." That's certainly not true. The law
   code had a perfectly legitimate function.
   Without its clear guidelines for right and
   wrong, moral behavior would be mostly
   guesswork. Apart from the succinct, sur-
   gical command, "You shall not covet,"
   I could have dressed covetousness up to
   look like a virtue and ruined my life
   with it.

Romans 7:7

Used the way it was intended by God, the law is
important: it shows us where we depart from
God's will. But when it is used to incite us to sin,
the whole thing is turned on its head.

Why is the law important for you?

PRAYER: Almighty and just Father, use your holy
commandments to show me where I miss the
mark, to expose my inability to be righteous on
my own, to awaken in me a dissatisfaction with
my own goodness, and to bring me to repentance. *Amen.*

"Cleverly Used to Trip Me Up"
Read Romans 7:9–12

> But once sin got its hands on the law code
> and decked itself out in all that finery,
> I was fooled, and fell for it. The very
> command that was supposed to guide
> me into life was cleverly used to trip me
> up, throwing me headlong.
>
> Romans 7:11

Just as an ax, fashioned to cut wood, can, when carelessly used, maim, and when maliciously used, kill, so the law, perfectly constructed, can be put to destructive uses.

Do you ever misuse the law?

PRAYER: God, I need far more than a surface knowledge of rules and regulations; I need a thorough understanding of your will in Jesus Christ. I need to know your word from the inside so that I can pursue your purpose for me in Christ. *Amen.*

"In Sin's Prison"

Read Romans 7:13–15

I can anticipate the response that is coming:
"I know that all God's commands are
spiritual, but I'm not. Isn't this also your
experience?" Yes. I'm full of myself—
after all, I've spent a long time in sin's
prison.

Romans 7:14

The Greeks said, "Know thyself." But who can do
it? It is like telling a man with a broken-down car
to understand without giving him a repair manual.
We know something is wrong with our lives—the
law tells us that. But we need help to understand
what is wrong and how it can be fixed.

What help do you need?

PRAYER: Blessed God, when I could not help myself you "lifted me out of the ditch, pulled me
from deep mud. You stood me up on a solid rock
to make sure I wouldn't slip" (Psalm 40:2). Thank
you in Jesus' name. *Amen.*

"I Can't Do It"
Read Romans 7:16–20

I realize that I don't have what it takes.
I can will it, but I can't do it.

Romans 7:18

The admission of inability is not evidence of a lazy person who won't work or a quitter who won't keep at it, but the soul-shattering realization that no matter how hard I try I cannot save myself.

What can't you do?

PRAYER: It is not more information that I need, Lord—I already know far more than I put to use. And it is not more desire that I need—my eyes are already bigger than my stomach. I need you to make me whole and keep me faithful. *Amen.*

MARCH 1

"Something Has Gone Wrong"
Read Romans 7:21–23

Something has gone wrong deep within
me and gets the better of me every time.

Romans 7:23

Balcony voices urge us on and call us upward to
God. Basement forces hold us back and pull us
downward to sin. We are pulled both ways.

Who speaks to you from the balcony?

PRAYER: I will not be naive, Lord, and suppose
that everything will turn out all right if I do my
best. And I will not be pessimistic, convinced that
sin will always get the best of me. I will believe that
you will do what I can never do for myself, in
Jesus. Amen.

MARCH 2

"The End of My Rope"
Read Romans 7:24–25

I've tried everything and nothing helps.
I'm at the end of my rope. Is there no
one who can do anything for me? Isn't
that the real question?

Romans 7:24

If we don't ask the right question we will never
understand ourselves. But if we don't hear the
right answer we will never realize God's ways with
us. The gospel forces us to attend to the right
question and prepares us to hear the right answer.

What is the question? What is the answer?

PRAYER: All thanks to you, great God, for making
me. All praise to you, dear Christ, for delivering me
from sin. All glory to you, Holy Spirit, for gifts to
live well. *Amen.*

MARCH 3

"Resolved"

Read Romans 8:1

With the arrival of Jesus, the Messiah, that
fateful dilemma is resolved. Those who
enter into Christ's being-here-for-us no
longer have to live under a continuous,
low-lying black cloud.

Romans 8:1

Jesus sockets what God does into our experience.
God's will has consequences in us. We live as a result of
the mighty work of God in Christ. We exist, not in
theory but in fact, acquitted.

What is the "fateful dilemma"?

PRAYER: God, thank you for this final word on my
destiny. There is much that I will never know, but
this is sure: my future with you is fixed and final.
Show me how to live my gratitude, through Jesus
Christ. Amen.

"Went for the Jugular"
Read Romans 8:2—4

God went for the jugular when he sent
his own Son. He didn't deal with the
problem as something remote and
unimportant. In his Son, Jesus, he
personally took on the human condition, entered the disordered mess of
struggling humanity in order to set it
right once and for all.

Romans 8:3

Instead of condemning me, God condemns sin.
The believing person is distinguished from the
disordered will. I am put on God's side in the battle against unbelief.

What are the results of Christ's work?

PRAYER: As I meditate the deep mysteries of redemption, O God, lead me into the sweeping clarity of faith. Make incomprehensible grace into the
plain speech and simple obedience of this day's
discipleship. *Amen.*

MARCH 5

"Focusing"

Read Romans 8:5–8

Focusing on the self is the opposite
of focusing on God.

Romans 8:6

Martin Luther once said that while we can't keep
the birds from landing on our heads, we can
prevent them from building nests in our hair.
Thoughts come and go, unbidden; meditation is
thought that is disciplined to exclude distractions,
paying attention to God's spirit only.

When do you meditate?

PRAYER: Very often, dear Christ, I am only wool-
gathering when I should be meditating, only day-
dreaming when I should be thinking. I dedicate
my mind to you to think your thoughts after you.
Amen.

"Taken Up Residence"

Read Romans 8:9–10

But if God himself has taken up residence
in your life, you can hardly be thinking
more of yourself than of him. Anyone,
of course, who has not welcomed this
invisible but clearly present God, the
Spirit of Christ, won't know what we're
talking about.

Romans 8:9

Christian faith is not an opinion about something
conjectured; it is an experience of new life within
the actual conditions of the body that is then lived
through the senses.

What are the implications here of "taken up
residence in your life"?

PRAYER: "Gracious Spirit, dwell with me; I myself
would gracious be; And with words that help and
heal Would Thy life in mine reveal; And with actions bold and meek Would for Christ my Saviour
speak" (Thomas Toke Lynch, "Gracious Spirit,
Dwell with Me," *The Hymnbook*, 241). *Amen.*

"Raised"

Read Romans 8:11

It stands to reason, doesn't it, that if the
alive-and-present God who raised Jesus
from the dead moves into your life, he'll
do the same thing in you that he did in
Jesus, bringing you alive to himself?
When God lives and breathes in you
(and he does, as surely as he did in
Jesus), you are delivered from that dead
life. With his Spirit living in you, your
body will be as alive as Christ's!

Romans 8:11

Resurrection is not a gossamer dream in a fantasy
future—it has to do with the material and physical realities of the present. God gives life where
and when I need it most: here and now.

How do you experience resurrection?

PRAYER: Risen Christ, raise me to new life each
morning. Grant that my speech and action may, by
the power of your Spirit, participate in your life
that conquers sin and defeats death. *Amen.*

MARCH 8

"Beckons"

Read Romans 8:12–14

God's Spirit beckons. There are things to
  do and places to go!

Romans 8:14

We do not wander, we are led. We determine to
respond to no one other than or contrary to the
Spirit of God. We hear his voice and take his direction. He sets the goals that shape and define
our daily tasks.

Where is the Spirit beckoning you?

PRAYER: God, I shut my ears to all who advise me
on how to be healthy, how to be successful, how
to get to heaven; I open my ears to you and attend
to the direction and guidance you provide in leading me to eternal life. *Amen.*

MARCH 9

"Papa"

Read Romans 8:15–17

This resurrection life you received from
God is not a timid, grave-tending life.
It's adventurously expectant, greeting
God with a childlike, "What's next,
Papa?" God's Spirit touches our spirits
and confirms who we really are. We
know who he is, and we know who we
are: Father and children. And we know
we are going to get what's coming to
us—an unbelievable inheritance!

Romans 8:15–16

God is not a problem but a relationship. We do
not figure him out, we speak and listen. Through
Christ we know that we are on intimate and
friendly terms with God—our Father whom we
respect in love.

What does it mean to be an heir?

PRAYER: Free me, Father, from all cringing fear
and from all cool intellectualism. Lead me into the
warm, personal trust that your Son has revealed as
my Savior. Amen.

"Hardly Wait"
Read Romans 8:18–21

The created world itself can hardly wait for
what's coming next.

Romans 8:19

The entire creation—animals and trees, oceans
and mountains—is on our side in anticipating the
completion of redemption. Personal faith sometimes is experienced as a lonely affair; in fact, it is
backed up by the entire creation!

What are the glorious times ahead?

PRAYER: I thank you, dear God, for the magnificent creation that anticipates, with me, the glorious consummation, when "the wilderness and
the dry land shall be glad, the desert shall rejoice
and blossom" (Isaiah 35:1). *Amen.*

"Pain Throughout the World"

Read Romans 8:22–25

All around us we observe a pregnant
creation. The difficult times of pain
throughout the world are simply birth
pangs.

Romans 8:22

We are in the middle of a great and arduous act of
creation—a bringing to birth of God's redemptive
love. Nothing is yet finished. Not only we ourselves, but everything around us is involved in the
new life that he is bringing into being.

How do you experience the birth pangs?

PRAYER: I thank you, God, that whatever pain I experience is part of a birth, not a death. Forbid that
I should ever become smug in my achievements
or despairing over my failures, knowing that you
are deeply at work in me and everyone to bring
about the new creation, in Christ. *Amen.*

MARCH 12

"Making Prayer"
Read Romans 8:26–27

Meanwhile, the moment we get tired
in the waiting, God's Spirit is right
alongside helping us along. If we don't
know how or what to pray, it doesn't
matter. He does our praying in and for
us, making prayer out of our wordless
sighs, our aching groans.

Romans 8:26

The Spirit shapes our unspoken longings and in-
articulate hungers into intercessions that God will
answer. We don't know what we need and we
don't know what God will do. We only know that
we need and that God will do what is necessary for
our salvation.

Why do you need the Spirit in your prayer?

PRAYER: Shape, O Holy Spirit, my confused and
stuttering speech into prayers that are pleasing to
the Father through Jesus Christ. *Amen.*

"Worked into Something Good"
Read Romans 8:28–30

That's why we can be so sure that every detail in our lives of love for God is worked into something good.

Romans 8:28

It is hard to believe, but it is true: nothing escapes God's attention and everything is used as a means to our final good. God is never against us and never indifferent to us, but always for us and in us.

Do you ever doubt that "every detail . . . is worked into something good"?

PRAYER: Forgive me, God, when I diminish you by my doubts and straitjacket you by my dogmatism. Even then you are undiminished and unconfined. Continue to do your good work in me, completing those purposes in which you have been "long beforehand with my soul"(Lynch, "I Sought the Lord, and Afterward I Knew," *The Hymnbook*, 402). *Amen.*

MARCH 14

"A Wedge?"

Read Romans 8:31–36

Do you think anyone is going to be able to
drive a wedge between us and Christ's
love for us? There is no way! Not trouble,
not hard times, not hatred, not hunger,
not homelessness, not bullying threats,
not backstabbing, not even the worst
sins listed in Scripture.

Romans 8:35

We are meticulous in adding up our troubles, in
taking the measure of adversity, in calculating
our survival chances in tribulation. But we always
leave out the most important reality—God. "Are
our tremors to measure the Omnipotence?"
(Charles Williams, *Descent of the Dove* [London: Lay-
mans, Green & Co., 1939], 5).

What fears get between you and God?

PRAYER: Keep me steadily aware of your powerful,
victorious, justifying presence in every part of my
life, O Christ, so that no timidity will turn me
back and no mistrust keep me from courageously
following you. *Amen.*

"Absolutely Nothing"
Read Romans 8:37–39

> I'm absolutely convinced that nothing—
> nothing living or dead, angelic or
> demonic, today or tomorrow, high
> or low, thinkable or unthinkable—
> absolutely nothing can get between us
> and God's love because of the way that
> Jesus our Master has embraced us.
>
> Romans 8:38–39

For the person who has become accustomed to just getting by, reduced to bare spiritual survival, Paul's witness is revolutionary: we are not desperately hanging on to God; God is holding on tenaciously to us!

What are some things that cannot separate you from God?

PRAYER: God, you replace all my fears with confidence. You banish timidity and install hope. You remove caution and create a venturesome faith. You affirm your love in every dimension of my life. Thank you! Amen.

"My Family"

Read Romans 9:1–5

If there were any way I could be cursed
by the Messiah so they could be blessed
by him, I'd do it in a minute. They're
my family. I grew up with them.

Romans 9:3

The gift of God's love in Christ is not a treasure to
be hoarded—Paul wants others in on it, too. Salvation is not a "me first" affair. There is no trace
of selfishness in this gospel.

Who is Paul's family?

PRAYER: God, while I am confident in your presence, I will not be indifferent toward those who
are still sunk in despair. I want to share what I
have received and persuade others of your good
salvation in Christ. Amen.

"God's Promise"

Read Romans 9:6–13

> It wasn't Abraham's sperm that gave
> identity here, but God's promise.
>
> Romans 9:8

God's call and promises are embedded in history, among actual people in locatable places, but they are never determined by blood ties. An accurate understanding of God's ways can never be pursued along strictly racial lines.

How many Old Testament quotations are cited here?

PRAYER: Father in heaven, give me an understanding of the ways in which you work in history, so that I will recognize your call and respond to your promises and so experience your elective purposes in my life. *Amen.*

"Moral Sweat"

Read Romans 9:14–18

Compassion doesn't originate in our
bleeding hearts or moral sweat, but
in God's mercy.

Romans 9:16

We cannot manipulate God. We cannot put him into our computers (or our theology) and use him. He is free. He makes the decisions and initiates the actions. But does that mean that he is capricious? "Not so fast, please."

Do you ever feel that God is unfair?

PRAYER: Deepen my faith, Lord, so that even when I don't understand your ways (especially when I don't understand your ways!) I will still praise you, knowing that you do all things right, in Jesus Christ. Amen.

"A Potter"

Read Romans 9:19–26

Clay doesn't talk back to the fingers that
mold it, saying, "Why did you shape me
like this?" Isn't it obvious that a potter
has a perfect right to shape one lump of
clay into a vase for holding flowers and
another into a pot for cooking beans?

Romans 9:21

That God is in complete control of salvation does
not mean that nothing we do makes any difference. On the contrary, everything we do, whether
glorious or menial, is significant, for God uses it
to work out his purposes.

What in your life seems insignificant?

PRAYER: Sovereign Lord, I will not proudly exempt myself from menial tasks. You have molded
my life for your purposes; now use me, however
you will, in Jesus Christ. *Amen.*

"Personal Selection"
Read Romans 9:27–29

Isaiah maintained this same emphasis: "If each grain of sand on the seashore were numbered and the sum labeled 'chosen of God,' they'd be numbers still, not names; salvation comes by personal selection."

Romans 9:27

God does not make decisions by adding up votes. We must not seek to be part of any majority—majorities are often wrong—but to be among those who do God's will, the remnant responsive to his mercy.

What is "personal selection"?

PRAYER: Lead me, Lord, into the inner intensities and finer disciplines of that small band of disciples who care more for your sentences than the world's propaganda. *Amen.*

"Stumbled"

Read Romans 9:30–33

How could they miss it? Because instead of
trusting God, they took over. They were
absorbed in what they themselves were
doing. They were so absorbed in their
"God projects" that they didn't notice
God right in front of them, like a huge
rock in the middle of the road. And so
they stumbled into him and went
sprawling.

Romans 9:32

There is no getting around Christ. He is there,
massive and unavoidable. We either accept him as
the foundation stone or painfully stumble over
him as we try to get to God on our own.

Where does Paul get his quotation?

PRAYER: God, I will no longer try to find my own
way to eternity. I will not build my own tower to
heaven. I accept what you have given in Jesus and
agree to let you build my life on his firm foundation. *Amen.*

"Don't Seem to Realize"
Read Romans 10:1–4

They don't seem to realize that this comprehensive setting-things-right that is
salvation is *God's* business, and a most
flourishing business it is. Right across
the street they set up their own salvation
shops and noisily hawk their wares.

Romans 10:3

Stepping on the accelerator doesn't get us to our
destination any faster if we are on the wrong road.
If we are doing the wrong thing, or doing something in the wrong way, increased zeal only makes
it worse.

Who were Paul's friends?

PRAYER: "Savior, like a Shepherd lead us, Much we
need Thy tender care; In Thy pleasant pastures feed
us, For our use Thy folds prepare: Blessed Jesus,
Blessed Jesus, Thou has bought us, Thine we are"
(Dorothy Thrupp, "Savior, Like a Shepherd Lead
Us," *The Hymnbook*, 380). *Amen.*

MARCH 23

"Everyone Who Calls"
Read Romans 10:5–13

Everyone who calls, "Help, God!"
gets help.

Romans 10:13

This marvelously succinct outline of the essentials
that are involved in a saved relationship with God
compresses a vast and complex reality into a brief,
pungent invitation.

What scripture does Paul quote?

PRAYER: Dear God, I don't want to get so bogged
down in the details of doctrine that I miss the
point of salvation, or so absorbed in examining
the trees of history that I miss the forest of faith.
Show me clearly the one thing needful, in Jesus.
Amen.

"How Can People Call?"
Read Romans 10:14–17

But how can people call for help if they
don't know who to trust? And how can
they know who to trust if they haven't
heard of the One who can be trusted?
And how can they hear if nobody tells
them?

Romans 10:14

The linked acts of sending, preaching, hearing,
believing, and calling are arranged by the Spirit
into a sequence that demonstrates how our call
for help to God is tied into God's provision of
help for us.

Who told you the good news?

PRAYER: Speak the word, O God, and provide
the preacher that will bring me the good news.
Awaken desire and kindle faith that will turn what
I hear into steady trust. *Amen.*

"Day After Day After Day"
Read Romans 10:18–21

Then he capped it with a damning
indictment: "Day after day after day,
I beckoned Israel with open arms,
and got nothing for my trouble but
cold shoulders and icy stares."

Romans 10:21

The great problem in communicating the gospel is not in its proclamation but in its reception. God's word has gone out boldly and clearly, but there has not been a willingness to listen. We don't need more and better *speakers* of God's word, but more and better *listeners* to it.

Do you listen as well as you speak?

PRAYER: Lord God, I would not blame any preacher for my disobedience nor fault any teacher with my ignorance. If I act and think wrongly, the error is more likely in my hearing than in their speaking. Help me to listen, attentively and in faith, for Jesus' sake. *Amen.*

"Choosing Them"

Read Romans 11:1–6

It's the same today. There's a fiercely loyal
minority still—not many, perhaps, but
probably more than you think. They're
holding on, not because of what they
think they're going to get out of it, but
because they're convinced of God's grace
and purpose in choosing them. If they
were only thinking of their own immediate self-interest, they would have left
long ago.

Romans 11:5

In one way, the entire Hebrew history looks like a
disaster, an attempt to get to God that never
worked. Another way to look at the same history
is that no matter how much we bungle the job,
God does not reject us—he continues to develop
righteousness by faith.

How could Paul be so sure that God had not rejected Israel?

PRAYER: I take comfort, dear God, in your long-
suffering with Israel and your persistence in choosing them even as they were choosing something
else. Be long-suffering and gracious with me also.
Amen.

"Self-Centered Ways"
Read Romans 11:7–10

Moses and Isaiah both commented on this:
> "Fed up with their quarrelsome, self-
> centered ways, God blurred their eyes
> and dulled their ears, Shut them in on
> themselves in a hall of mirrors, and
> they're there to this day."

Romans 11:8

No one could be defiant of grace and scornful of faith and retain an aptitude for the things of God. Unbelief produces its own rewards: those who refuse to believe, become, finally, unable to believe.

How do you avoid "quarrelsome, self-centered ways"?

PRAYER: Lord, keep me awake to every word you speak, watchful for the morning, alert to temptation, alive to your spirit, so that my praise may be lively and my steps straight. In Jesus' name. *Amen.*

"What a Homecoming!"
Read Romans 11:11–12

> Now, if their leaving triggered this
> worldwide coming of non-Jewish
> outsiders to God's kingdom, just
> imagine the effect of their coming
> back! What a homecoming!
>
> Romans 11:12

No one should draw premature conclusions about anyone's final damnation. Falling is not the necessary consequence of stumbling. Nobody can be "written off" in matters of salvation.

Restate Paul's argument.

PRAYER: As I, Lord, love my neighbors, help me to be their keepers and not their critics. When I see them lose their way I would not turn away from them in disgust but toward them in intercession; in the name of Jesus, that great shepherd of the sheep. *Amen.*

"First Thing"
Read Romans 11:13–16

> If the first thing the Jews did, even though
> it was wrong for them, turned out for
> your good, just think what's going to
> happen when they get it right!
>
> Romans 11:16

Paul's special vocation to the Gentiles did not divert him from concern for his own Hebrew family: he was continually grateful for their place ("the first thing") in the scheme of salvation and compassionately hopeful for their salvation ("their recovery").

What do you owe to Jesus?

PRAYER: Almighty Savior, make my calling clear to me so that I may, without hesitation, proceed to keep your commands, whether at home or at work, with my family and with my friends, here or away. *Amen.*

"Other Branches"

Read Romans 11:17–24

It's certainly possible to say, "Other branches were pruned so that I could be grafted in!" Well and good. But they were pruned because they were deadwood, no longer connected by belief and commitment to the root. The only reason you're on the tree is because your graft "took" when you believed, and because you're connected to that belief-nurturing root. So don't get cocky and strut your branch. Be humbly mindful of the root that keeps you lithe and green.

Romans 11:17–18

We cannot define our good fortune at the expense of someone else's exclusion. Anti-Semitism (or anti-anything) is intolerable among people who have been received by grace. The only proper response for those who find themselves grafted into the tree of salvation is awe.

Who were the "branches"?

PRAYER: In adoration, awe, and wonder, O God, I meditate on your ways. As I grow, may it always be in order to look up to you in gratitude and never down on others in pride. Amen.

"This Is Complicated"
Read Romans 11:25–32

I want to lay all this out on the table as
clearly as I can, friends. This is complicated. It would be easy to misinterpret
what's going on and arrogantly assume
that you're royalty and they're just rabble,
out on their ears for good. But that's not it
at all. This hardness on the part of insider
Israel toward God is temporary. Its effect
is to open things up to all the outsiders
so that we end up with a full house.

Romans 11:25

Can God save Israel in the face of her disobedience? He can and he will. There is no limit in
God's will to save. The range of his love is bound-
less, the depth of his patience is bottomless, the
reach of his grace is endless.

How does this passage make you feel?

PRAYER: "Depth of mercy! Can there be Mercy still
reserved for me? Can my God His wrath forbear?
Me, the chief of sinners, spare? Still for me the
Saviour stands, Shows His wounds, and spreads
His hands; God is love! I know, I feel; Jesus weeps,
and loves me still" (Charles Wesley, "Depth of
Mercy! Can There Be," *The Hymnbook*, 273). *Amen.*

APRIL 1

"Deep, Deep Wisdom!"
Read Romans 11:33–36

Have you ever come on anything quite like
this extravagant generosity of God, this
deep, deep wisdom? It's way over our
heads. We'll never figure it out.

Romans 11:33

The surprises in God always have to do with finding more, not less. The mysteries in God are not
mysteries of darkness but of light. They do not
hide furtive secrets but dazzle our minds with lu-
minous reality.

In what ways have you been surprised by God?

PRAYER: Glorious Christ: what a vast country of
truth and experience to explore by your Spirit!
Each day opens up new vistas; each step discovers
new gifts. Thank you for being so much more
than I had ever guessed or hoped. Amen.

"Ordinary Life"

Read Romans 12:1

So here's what I want you to do, God
helping you: Take your everyday,
ordinary life—your sleeping, eating,
going-to-work, and walking-around
life—and place it before God as an
offering. Embracing what God does
for you is the best thing you can do
for him.

Romans 12:1

"Only connect" (E. M. Forster). What we believe
connects with the way we live. Heart responses
result in body action. Paul knew nothing of a religion of spirit divorced from the bone and muscle
of everyday life.

Do you think your body is as important as your
soul?

PRAYER: Lord Jesus Christ, your body centered the
entire love of God in acts of speech and healing,
suffering and salvation. Use my body also to bring
into being what you intend for love. *Amen.*

APRIL 3

"From the Inside Out"

Read Romans 12:2

Don't become so well-adjusted to your
culture that you fit into it without even
thinking. Instead, fix your attention on
God. You'll be changed from the inside
out. Readily recognize what he wants
from you, and quickly respond to it.
Unlike the culture around you, always
dragging you down to its level of imma-
turity, God brings the best out of you,
develops well-formed maturity in you.

Romans 12:2

We can be shaped, like a cookie cutter shapes
dough, to fit what the crowd expects of us; or we
can be shaped, like a seed shapes a flower, into a
unique instance of living beauty.

What is the most powerful shaping force on
you?

PRAYER: I know, O Christ, that your Spirit is in me
to develop and mature your will in me: show me
how to resist the conforming powers of the world
and respond to the transforming powers of your
will. *Amen.*

APRIL 4

"God Brings It All"
Read Romans 12:3

I'm speaking to you out of deep gratitude
for all that God has given me, and especially as I have responsibilities in relation
to you. Living then, as every one of you
does, in pure grace, it's important that
you not misinterpret yourselves as
people who are bringing this goodness
to God. No, God brings it all to you.
The only accurate way to understand
ourselves is by what God is and by what
he does for us, not by what we are and
what we do for him.

Romans 12:3

No one is like another: God has a design for each
of us for which he provides guidance and assistance and help. We don't have to guess our way
through life to find our place; we can believe our
way into the person he wants us to be.

Are you satisfied with how well you know
yourself?

PRAYER: Help me, God, to quit comparing myself
with others, always feeling either inferior or superior. Help me to see myself loved and directed
by you, realizing what is special in me and what
my life means to you. *Amen.*

"Its Meaning"

Read Romans 12:4—5

> In this way we are like the various parts of a
> human body. Each part gets its meaning
> from the body as a whole, not the other
> way around.

Romans 12:4

The gospel truth that Paul is arguing can come as
no surprise to anyone who carefully observes the
creation: our very bodies are outward evidence of
the truth. There is great variety in our appearance
and abilities, but a common purpose coordinat-
ing every part.

What is your meaning?

PRAYER: I look at the world around me, O Christ,
and see this incredible diversity, but know that it
is not random and accidental. Lead me to accept
my own place in all of this as planned and essential, a detail on which you lavish much care! Amen.

"Functioning Parts"

Read Romans 12:6–8

> So since we find ourselves fashioned into
> all these excellently formed and mar-
> velously functioning parts in Christ's
> body, let's just go ahead and be what
> we were made to be, without enviously
> or pridefully comparing ourselves with
> each other, or trying to be something
> we aren't.
>
> Romans 12:6–7

The word is not "jobs" but "functioning parts." Paul's insight is not that we have this enormous task to do and must all take our part; it is that we have this amazing life to live and all are invited to participate in it.

How many gifts or functioning parts does Paul name?

PRAYER: "We give Thee but Thine own, Whate'er the gift may be: All that we have is Thine alone, A trust, O Lord, from Thee" (William Walsham How, "We Give Thee but Thine Own," *The Hymnbook*, 312). *Amen.*

APRIL 7

"Fueled and Aflame"
Read Romans 12:9–13

Don't burn out; keep yourselves fueled and
aflame. Be alert servants of the Master,
cheerfully expectant.

Romans 12:11

The characteristic attitude in living a gift-life is
one of being aflame in the spirit. There is nothing
plodding or grudging here. When we see our
lives permeated by grace and mercy, we are free to
respond in freedom and joy.

Which command suits you for today?

PRAYER: I am, Lord, often sluggish. Rescue me
from the quagmire of my feelings of self-pity and
set me on the firm ground of your gospel, so that
I can dance my way through the day, delighting in
what you provide for me to do in Christ's name.
Amen.

"Bless"

Read Romans 12:14–21

Bless your enemies; no cursing under your
breath.

Romans 12:14

God is for us, therefore we can be for everyone we
meet. It is no longer our responsibility to get rid
of evil; God has done the definitive job on that at
the cross. Now it is our privilege to share goodness—gladly witnessing, cheerfully helping.

Whom will you bless today?

PRAYER: I am very good at telling people what I
don't like about them, Father. Train me today in
discovering what you like about them and then
telling them! *Amen.*

"He Uses Them"
Read Romans 13:1–5

God also has an interest in keeping order,
and he uses them to do it. That's why
you must live responsibly—not just to
avoid punishment but also because it's
the right way to live.

Romans 13:4

God is over us: he is the fundamental and final
authority. But that does not exempt us from living responsibly under interim authorities such as
governments. Earthly authorities, when they do
not command what is evil, can be good training
in obedience to divine sovereignty.

What obedience is difficult for you?

PRAYER: When I try to avoid the authority of others so that I can get my own way, show me, O
God, how I can practice the skills of submission
by which my will becomes responsive to the truth
of another, and so become responsive to you.
Amen.

"Fulfill Your Obligations"
Read Romans 13:6–7

Fulfill your obligations as a citizen. Pay
your taxes, pay your bills, respect your
leaders.

Romans 13:7

Because we Christians have our primary citizenship in heaven and our first allegiance to our sovereign Lord, Christ our King, there always seem to be some among us who act as if they can't be bothered with the responsibilities of this world. It's an attitude that gets no encouragement from Paul—or Jesus.

Read what Jesus says about this in Mark 11:13–17.

PRAYER: Christ my King, I want to serve you with everything that I am and have. But don't ever let me use my commitment to you as an excuse for getting sloppy with my earthly duties. I want the working of your will in me to be as evident "on earth as it is in heaven" (Matthew 6:10). Amen.

"Adds Up"

Read Romans 13:8–10

> The law code—don't sleep with another
> person's spouse, don't take someone's
> life, don't take what isn't yours, don't
> always be wanting what you don't have,
> and any other "don't" you can think
> of—finally adds up to this: Love other
> people as well as you do yourself.
>
> Romans 13:9

Lest we become bogged down in the details of morality, we need occasional breaks from our routines so that we can see the whole picture: "Love other people" makes overall sense out of the hundred obligations and prohibitions that are involved in daily relationships.

Who are the "other people"?

PRAYER: Too many times, Lord, I use my moral behavior to demonstrate that I am better than others. I need your help to use it as an instrument of love, so that others are brought near by my conduct and not put off, and find evidence of a warm love, not a cool self-righteousness. *Amen.*

APRIL 12

"Be Up and Awake"
Read Romans 13:11–14

The night is about over, dawn is about to
   break. Be up and awake to what God
   is doing! God is putting the finishing
   touches on the salvation work he began
   when we first believed.

Romans 13:12

Christians are not vulnerable innocents: trust and
morality are invincible defenses. We only have to
be up and awake to what is provided for us and
we are equipped to withstand any assault of evil
and perform any feat of faith.

Compare this with Ephesians 6:10–20.

PRAYER: "Lead on, O King Eternal: We follow, not
with fears; For gladness breaks like morning
Where'er Thy face appears; Thy cross is lifted o'er
us; We journey in its light: The crown awaits the
conquest; Lead on, O God of might" (Ernest W.
Shurtleff, "Lead On, O King Eternal," The Hymnbook, 332). Amen.

"But Weak"

Read Romans 14:1—4

Welcome with open arms fellow believers
   who don't see things the way you do.
   And don't jump all over them every time
   they do or say something you don't
   agree with—even when it seems that
   they are strong on opinions but weak in
   the faith department.

Romans 14:1

At any one moment various people are at different
stages in the faith journey, some strong and running, others weak and faltering. The strong don't
help the weak by criticizing them or demanding
that they run faster.

Do you despise weak Christians?

PRAYER: Lord, you always had a special interest in
the despised, the rejected, and the left out. Give
me a similar sensitivity to those who experience
the contempt of the successful, and show me how
to share your mercy. *Amen.*

"To the Glory of God"

Read Romans 14:5–6

What's important in all this is that if you
keep a holy day, keep it for God's sake; if
you eat meat, eat it to the glory of God
and thank God for prime rib; if you're a
vegetarian, eat vegetables to the glory of
God and thank God for broccoli. None
of us is permitted to insist on our own
way in these matters.

Romans 14:6

A rigid insistence that all honor the Lord in precisely the same way dishonors the Lord. There are
many details in Christian behavior in which differences are allowed. We are under the same con-
ductor, but we do not all play the same notes.

Do you have fellowship with those with whom
you differ?

PRAYER: God, help me to appreciate the ways others express their love for you. Grant that I, though
different, may be in tune with them so that together our praise of your name may be harmo-
nious. *Amen.*

"Our Master"

Read Romans 14:7–9

> That's why Jesus lived and died and then
> lived again: so that he could be our
> Master across the entire range of life
> and death, and free us from the petty
> tyrannies of each other.
>
> Romans 14:8

The most important thing about us is not who we are in ourselves but who we are in relationship to God. The gospel is not an exclusive club from which I can bar God; nor is my salvation a private affair from which I can exclude others.

What is wrong with private religion?

PRAYER: Free me, Christ, from the narrow confines of my sin so that I can enter the wide-open fields of your redemption, discovering the liberty of living by your creative will, among others whom you love and lead. *Amen.*

"The Place of Judgment"
Read Romans 14:10–12

> So where does that leave you when you
> criticize a brother? And where does that
> leave you when you condescend to a
> sister? I'd say it leaves you looking pretty
> silly—or worse. Eventually, we're all
> going to end up kneeling side by side
> in the place of judgment, facing God.
>
> Romans 14:10

Only God is competent to see through our mixed motives and decide what has worth and what hasn't. And he will do it. It is work he does not delegate. For any of us to pretend to know what he will do finally is the height of presumption.

Do you pass judgment on your brother and sister?

PRAYER: God, break me of my bad habit of judging others, of drawing conclusions about them from insufficient data, and of making up my mind about them when I should be cultivating an appreciation for them. *Amen.*

"Don't Get in the Way"
Read Romans 14:13–14

Forget about deciding what's right for
each other. Here's what you need to be
concerned about: that you don't get in
the way of someone else, making life
more difficult than it already is.

Romans 14:13

Words of criticism and acts of rejection, gestures
of contempt and attitudes of condescension are
stones for others to trip over, and may lead to in-
juries far more serious than we suppose.

What criticisms have caused you to stumble?

PRAYER: "Investigate my life, O God, find out
everything about me; Cross-examine and test me,
get a clear picture of what I'm about; See for
yourself whether I've done anything wrong—
then guide me on the road to eternal life" (Psalm
139:23–24). *Amen.*

"Soul-Poisoning"
Read Romans 14:15–18

If you confuse others by making a big issue
over what they eat or don't eat, you're
no longer a companion with them in
love, are you? These, remember, are
persons for whom Christ died. Would
you risk sending them to hell over an
item in their diet? Don't you dare let a
piece of God-blessed food become an
occasion of soul-poisoning!

Romans 14:15

If I, in the name of faith and freedom, act in a way
that causes another to be diminished or destroyed,
my action can hardly be pleasing to God who loves
us both.

Are you sensitive to the way others respond to
you?

PRAYER: Dear Lord, I need your wisdom so that
my necessary concerns with food and drink are
handled in ways that do not obscure, contradict,
or interfere with your central realities of "setting
it right, putting it together, and completing it
with joy." *Amen.*

"Let's Agree"
Read Romans 14:19–21

So let's agree to use all our energy in
getting along with each other.

Romans 14:19

"Religion" must never be used as a weapon to cut
others down, or as a procedure to put them in
their places, but always as a passion to bring about
wholeness and build up maturity in Christ.

Is it obvious to others that you use your energy
in getting along with others?

PRAYER: "Let there be light, Lord God of Hosts, Let
there be wisdom on the earth; Let broad humanity
have birth, Let there be deeds, instead of boasts.
Give us the peace of vision clear To see our broth-
ers' good our own, To joy and suffer not alone—
The love that casteth out all fear" (William Merrill
Vories, "Let There Be Light, Lord God of Hosts,"
The Hymnbook, 480). Amen.

"Consistent"

Read Romans 14:22–23

> But if you're not sure, if you notice that
> you are acting in ways inconsistent with
> what you believe—some days trying to
> impose your opinions on others, other
> days just trying to please them—then
> you know that you're out of line. If the
> way you live isn't consistent with what
> you believe, then it's wrong.
>
> Romans 14:23

Any time we separate an item of truth or an article of behavior from a living relationship with God, it becomes a sin. We cannot take what is right and go off and use it any way we wish—it is God's truth and must be used in relation to his living will.

How do you apply this to your life?

PRAYER: When my knowledge of you gets separated from my love for you, show me my failure of faith, O God, and restore me quickly to wholeness. Keep me centered in your love, immersed in your will, and concerned for your ways, in Jesus' name. *Amen.*

"Most Convenient for Us"
Read Romans 15:1—4

Those of us who are strong and able in the
faith need to step in and lend a hand to
those who falter, and not just do what is
most convenient for us.

Romans 15:1

In an age when "me first" is sanctioned by our
psychologies and institutionalized in our economics, it is difficult (but all the more necessary)
to stand against the stream. The example of Christ
and the instruction of scripture make it possible
for us to do it.

What scripture does Paul quote?

PRAYER: I am a bundle of demands and desires,
God: I want to be at the center. Only by your grace
am I able to be happy with you at the center, and
content to share your concern for my neighbors.
Amen.

"In Harmony"

Read Romans 15:5–6

Then we'll be a choir—not our voices only,
    but our very lives singing in harmony
    in a stunning anthem to the God and
    Father of our Master Jesus!

Romans 15:6

We are given, as Christians, different instruments to play and different sounds to make. When we are in tune with the will of God and directed by the love of God, we are a symphony to the glory of God.

What musical instrument is your life most like?

PRAYER: "Forgive, O Lord, our severing ways, The rival altars that we raise, The wrangling tongues that mar Thy praise. A Sweeter song shall then be heard, Confessing, in a world's accord, The inward Christ, the living Word. That song shall swell from shore to shore, One hope, one faith, one love restore The seamless robe that Jesus wore" (John Greenleaf Whittier, "Forgive, O Lord, Our Severing Ways," *The Hymnbook*, 476). Amen.

"Welcome One Another"

Read Romans 15:7–13

So reach out and welcome one another to
God's glory. Jesus did it; now you do it!

Romans 15:7

The community of faith is the most open, accepting group of people on earth. Even a hint of snob-
bery or exclusivity is a scandal and must be
eliminated quickly. Those who have experienced
the generosity of Christ's welcome know how to
welcome others.

Who welcomed you into the community of
faith?

PRAYER: Lord, I want to share the same cheerful
and generous welcome with others that you gave
me. Help me to overcome barriers of reserve and
bridge chasms of loneliness so that others may experience your acceptance in Jesus Christ. *Amen.*

APRIL 24

"Underlining"
Read Romans 15:14–16

So, my dear friends, don't take my rather
bold and blunt language as criticism. It's
not criticism. I'm simply underlining
how very much I need your help in
carrying out this highly focused assignment God gave me.

Romans 15:15

Some people hear criticism in every suggestion—
and then bristle defensively, preventing further
conversation. Paul interprets his pastoral counsel
as "simply underlining." By writing to the Roman
Christians he is not implying that they are inferior
to all others but simply in need of what all of us
need—guidance and encouragement.

Compare verse 16 with chapter 12, verses 1–2.

PRAYER: For the most part, Lord, I don't need more
knowledge but more obedience. I am not puzzled
about *what* to do but simply slow in getting up to
do it. Prod my faith with Paul's reminders so that I
may run in the way you have set for me, in Jesus.
Amen.

"Proud"

Read Romans 15:17–21

> Looking back over what has been accomplished and what I have observed, I must say I am most pleased—in the context of Jesus, I'd even say proud, but only in that context.
>
> Romans 15:17

There is a difference between boastfully displaying achievements and accomplishments in order to appear important before others, and appreciating God's grace in allowing us to share in his work so that he will be glorified.

What are you proud of?

PRAYER: "My soul makes its boast in the Lord; let the humble hear and be glad. O magnify the Lord with me, and let us exalt his name together" (Psalm 34:2–3). *Amen.*

"Looked Forward"

Read Romans 15:22–24

And that's why it has taken me so long to
finally get around to coming to you. But
now that there is no more pioneering
work to be done in these parts, and
since I have looked forward to seeing
you for many years, I'm planning my
visit.

Romans 15:23

By setting God's will first and his own second,
Paul had both the satisfaction of seeing God's
work prosper and the pleasure of having his own
desires completed. God doesn't very often fulfill
our longings at the moment we want him to, but
he does finally complete our joy.

What personal goals have taken you "so long"
in meeting?

PRAYER: Father, what I want from you and what
you want from me are not the same. Show me
your will so that I may do that, and keep me open
to receive all that you give to make me whole so
that I may live in peace and joy. *Amen.*

"Take Up a Collection"

Read Romans 15:25–29

> The Greeks— all the way from the
> Macedonians in the north to the
> Achaians in the south—decided they
> wanted to take up a collection for
> the poor among the believers in
> Jerusalem.
>
> Romans 15:26

When it was discovered that the Christians in Jerusalem were poor and in need, the Greek Christians were immediately eager to relieve those needs. The way we spend our money is an expression of faith.

Whom do you want to help with your money?

PRAYER: "All things are Thine; no gift have we, Lord of all gifts, to offer Thee; And hence with grateful hearts today Thine own before Thy feet we lay" (John Greenleaf Whittier, "All Things Are Thine; No Gift Have We," *The Hymnbook*, 313). *Amen.*

"Earnest Prayer"
Read Romans 15:30–35

I appeal to you, brothers and sisters, by our
   Lord Jesus Christ and by the love of the
   Spirit, to join me in earnest prayer to
   God on my behalf.

Romans 15:30

Prayer is the strongest help we can give one who
is in danger or in need. Our prayers are the means
by which God brings about deliverance, provides
protection, opens doors of acceptance, and re-
leases joy. Nothing else we do counts as much.

   Who prays for you?

PRAYER: Lord Jesus Christ, your prayers for others
brought them through danger and preserved them
in temptation: grant that I also may be faithful in
prayer for those I know who are going through
difficult times and faced with arduous tasks. *Amen.*

APRIL 29

"She's Helped Many a Person"
Read Romans 16:1–2

Be sure to welcome our friend Phoebe
in the way of the Master, with all the
generous hospitality we Christians are
famous for. I heartily endorse both her
and her work. She's a key representative
of the church at Cenchrea. Help her out
in whatever she asks. She deserves anything you can do for her. She's helped
many a person, including me.

Romans 16:1–2

Phoebe seems to have made it her special ministry
to take charge of those foreigners who found
themselves without resources in Cenchrea, the
port city of Corinth.

What form of ministry are you good at?

PRAYER: Lord, help me to be alert and responsive
to the opportunities all around me to express your
love and exhibit your compassion in the name
and for the sake of Jesus Christ. *Amen.*

"Hello to . . ."

Read Romans 16:3–16

Say hello to Priscilla and Aquila, who
have worked hand in hand with me
in serving Jesus.

Romans 16:3

The "Romans" to whom Paul was writing were
not an abstract, faceless mob—all the time, Paul
had in mind particular people whose personal
names he knew well. No teaching and no preaching
is complete until it is addressed, by name, to
particular people.

How many names are mentioned in the list?

PRAYER: I thank you, God, for speaking my name
in love and singling me out for salvation. In turn, I
want to learn to greet every person I meet with the
same attention, concern, and gratitude in which I
have been addressed by you, in Jesus. *Amen.*

"A Wide Berth"

Read Romans 16:17–23

One final word of counsel, friends. Keep
a sharp eye out for those who take
bits and pieces of the teaching that you
learned and then use them to make
trouble. Give these people a wide berth.

Romans 16:17

The Christian community is characterized by its
greetings—a quickness to address each person
with the joy and acceptance of Christ. At the same
time, though, we are taught to be careful and
wary of any who are willfully malicious.

"Hospitable" does not mean "gullible."

Who takes bits and pieces of the teaching and
"uses them to make trouble" in the church today?

PRAYER: Give me, Lord, a discerning spirit so that
I may be able to distinguish between good and
evil, and know whom to greet and whom to give
wide berth. *Amen.*

"This Incomparably *Wise* God"
Read Romans 16:25–27

All our praise is focused through Jesus on
this incomparably wise God! Yes! *Amen.*

Romans 16:27

Paul's last word is not a profound teaching, not a
cheerful greeting, not a pressing admonition; it
is a prayer, setting each person in the community
of faith in the strength and under the command
of God.

What is the basis of Paul's final prayer?

PRAYER: Lord Jesus Christ, what glorious truth
you have revealed; what clear pathways you have
provided; what urgent motivations you have created! Now put it all together in me in a good life
of "obedient belief." *Amen.*

"Have Been Called"

Read 1 Corinthians 1:1

I, Paul, have been called and sent by Jesus,
the Messiah, according to God's plan,
along with my friend Sosthenes.

1 Corinthians 1:1

Paul, our greatest teacher and preacher, did not speak out of his own genius or write from his own wisdom. He was called and sent—removed from his own self-willed ways and launched into the orbit of redemption.

Why do you like Paul?

PRAYER: God, create in me a listening ear and a teachable spirit. Use your servant Paul to guide me in the ways of grace and to be responsive to the winds of the Spirit. *Amen.*

"God's Church at Corinth"

Read 1 Corinthians 1:2

I send this letter to you in God's church
at Corinth, Christians cleaned up by
Jesus and set apart for a God-filled life.
I include in my greeting all who call
out to Jesus, wherever they live. He's
their Master as well as ours!

1 Corinthians 1:2

The Greek seaport city of Corinth was a cross sec-
tion of the world. Every sort and condition of person and every degree of alienation from God
could be found there. Could God make a church
out of such unlikely people? Would he? He could
and he would.

How is our world similar to Corinth?

PRAYER: Lord, if you did it in Corinth, you can do
it where I live—with the sinners in my house, on
my street, in my church. Complete your work in
us. Make saints of us. *Amen.*

"Gifts and Benefits"

Read 1 Corinthians 1:3

May all the gifts and benefits that come
from God our Father and our Master,
Jesus Christ, be yours.

1 Corinthians 1:3

Overuse and underexperience have dulled and
made banal the two glorious gospel words ("grace
and peace"/"gifts and benefits"). Each time they
appear on the biblical page there is an explosion of
energy and light.

What is your experience with these words?

PRAYER: Christ, you come to me freely, unexpected,
surprising me out of my sin. You live with me generously,
sharing your wholeness and filling my
emptiness. Thank you for gifts and benefits. *Amen.*

MAY 6

"All God's Gifts"
Read 1 Corinthians 1:4–8

Just think—you don't need a thing, you've
   got it all! All God's gifts are right in front
   of you as you wait expectantly for our
   Master Jesus to arrive on the scene for
   the Finale.

1 Corinthians 1:7

One long-term experience among people of faith
is of *adequacy*—an inner, continuous *receiving* relationship with a *giving* God. In a society where
many are pitied and many are resented, the Christian is an instance of thanks.

What do you have in abundance?

PRAYER: I give thanks, O God, for the way you
have changed the lives of people I know and love.
Among them I thank you for ___. What extraordi-
nary blessings! What superb and sufficient gifts!
All praise! *Amen.*

"Got You Started . . . , Shares"

Read 1 Corinthians 1:9

God, who got you started in this spiritual
adventure, shares with us the life of his
Son and our Master Jesus. He will never
give up on you. Never forget that.

1 Corinthians 1:9

The foundation of the Christian life is not our
faithfulness to God, but his faithfulness to us. That
is what is unshakable. When we realize that and
respond to it, we experience faith and become
faithful.

How does God share with you the life of his
Son?

PRAYER: "Great is thy faithfulness, O God my Fa-
ther, There is no shadow of turning with thee.
All I have needed thy hand hath provided, Great
is thy faithfulness, O God, to me!" (Thomas O.
Chisholm, "Great Is Thy Faithfulness," Hymns II,
InterVarsity Press, 12). Amen.

"Fighting"
Read 1 Corinthians 1:10–17

I bring this up because some from Chloe's
family brought a most disturbing report
to my attention—that you're fighting
among yourselves!

1 Corinthians 1:11

When people don't get along, they very often try
to dignify their differences with spiritual reasons.
That is nonsense, says Paul. If we fight it is because of our sin, not because we are devoted to
some noble cause.

What fighting do you indulge in?

PRAYER: Forgive, O Christ, my shortsighted and
self-willed ways: for thinking that because I am
different, I am better; for claiming that since I have
a truth, I own all the truth. Make me one with all
your children, and coordinate us in love. *Amen.*

"What the World Considered Dumb"
Read 1 Corinthians 1:18–25

Since the world in all its fancy wisdom
  never had a clue when it came to
  knowing God, God in his wisdom
  took delight in using what the world
  considered dumb—preaching, of all
  things!—to bring those who trust him
  into the way of salvation.

1 Corinthians 1:21

The use of intelligence to get to God (the way of some Greeks) and the demand for the miraculous to manipulate God (the way of some Jews) continue to fail. The way of the cross, in which God comes to us and forgives us, however outlandish it may seem, has the overwhelming advantage that it works.

Why does God's way seem dumb?

PRAYER: God in Christ, crucified for my sins and raised for my salvation, continue your wise and miraculous work in me, showing your marvelous will and sharing your abundant life. *Amen.*

"Chose These 'Nobodies'"
Read 1 Corinthians 1:26–29

> Isn't it obvious that God deliberately chose
> men and women that the culture over-
> looks and exploits and abuses, chose
> these "nobodies" to expose the hollow
> pretensions of the "somebodies"?
>
> 1 Corinthians 1:28

Always, the central human problem is arrogance—
the prideful assumption that we can do without
God. The gospel starts at the opposite pole, with
the most vulnerable infant, the most despised
criminal (the Bethlehem cradle, the Jerusalem
cross), and proclaims the new humanity that lives
in adoration and faith in God.

How does boasting differ from praising?

PRAYER: God, you lead me into unaccustomed
paths of ordinariness and show me the splendor
of your presence. You take me into the society of
people I had supposed were losers and show me
their beauties and strengths. Thank you, O God,
for starting with me where I am and taking me to
where you are. *Amen.*

MAY 11

"Comes from God"
Read 1 Corinthians 1:30–31

Everything that we have— right thinking
and right living, a clean slate and a fresh
start—comes from God by way of Jesus
Christ.

1 Corinthians 1:30

If we are to live well, it is essential that we start in
the right place: Jesus Christ is the source of all aspects of life that make it whole and complete and
good. From him we get life in its purest form.

Compare this with Jeremiah 9:23–24.

PRAYER: Eternal and gracious Father, I give you
thanks for providing me with all that I need in
Jesus. I praise you for wholeness and fullness in
him. Keep me ever close to my source, and grateful. Amen.

"Jesus Crucified"

Read 1 Corinthians 2:1–2

> I deliberately kept it plain and simple: first
> Jesus and who he is; then Jesus and what
> he did—Jesus crucified.
>
> 1 Corinthians 2:2

We are always attempting to turn the message of Jesus Christ into a story about a fine man, or a great man, or an interesting man. Paul steadily insisted that it was the story of God and a demonstration of the way God enters into our lives in sacrifice and resurrection.

Why is humanity's wisdom misleading?

PRAYER: God, set the crucified always before me: evidence of what *you* do and not what I do, so that I am attentive to your salvation and not my achievements, interested in the completely adequate way you deal with me and not in the always inadequate ways I deal with you. *Amen.*

"Scared to Death"
Read 1 Corinthians 2:3–5

I was unsure of how to go about this, and
felt totally inadequate—I was scared to
death, if you want the truth of it—and
so nothing I said could have impressed
you or anyone else.

1 Corinthians 2:3

Paul freely confessed that he was scared to death.
The power of the gospel does not come from
spokespeople who pretend to a confidence that
they don't have, or who put up a front of bravado
to hide inner insecurities. It is enough that we
simply witness to the crucified.

How do you acquire confidence?

PRAYER: Father, I confess that sometimes faith for
me is only "putting up a good front." I would be
more honest if I admitted to being "scared to
death." Even while I am frightened, Lord, keep
me faithful and mindful that victory comes not by
might nor by power but by your spirit. *Amen.*

"Into the Open"
Read 1 Corinthians 2:6–10

But you've seen and heard it because God by
his Spirit has brought it all out into the
open before you.

1 Corinthians 2:10

Just because the gospel is plain and modest does
not mean that it is shallow or simplistic. There are
heights and depths in God into which the Spirit
guides us in a lifetime of faith-exploration.

Read Isaiah 64:4.

PRAYER: Thank you, God, for telling me the secret—for letting me in on the love plans and salvation plots that you are working out in Christ.
Thank you for giving me the inside story. *Amen.*

MAY 15

"Learned It from God"
Read 1 Corinthians 2:11–13

We didn't learn this by reading books or
    going to school; we learned it from
    God, who taught us person-to-person
    through Jesus, and we're passing it on to
    you in the same firsthand, personal way.
                                1 Corinthians 2:13

The way in which we learn the new life in Christ is
as important as *what* we learn. It is not so much
the mastery of certain ideas as the development of
a relationship. Only by the Holy Spirit can our
ideas and our faith be coordinated in such a way
that we live comprehending God.

How does the Spirit teach?

PRAYER: God, I accept your Holy Spirit as my
teacher. As he teaches and I learn, may all my
knowing and my doing flow from a center of
being that is created and sustained by you, in
Christ. *Amen.*

"Silliness"
Read 1 Corinthians 2:14–15

The unspiritual self, just as it is by nature,
  can't receive the gifts of God's Spirit.
  There's no capacity for them. They
  seem like so much silliness. Spirit can
  be known only by spirit—God's Spirit
  and our spirits in open communion.

1 Corinthians 2:14

For people who set themselves at the center and whose goal is to control others, acquire goods, and indulge the passions, the gospel is the rankest nonsense. No arguments will make it otherwise. From another point of view (from Sinai and Calvary), it is the richest wisdom.

What does it mean to be unspiritual?

PRAYER: I am so gullible and uncritical, Lord! So many experts to tell me how to diet and exercise and think and enjoy and get ahead! I let everyone tell me what is best for me. All along, though, what I really want is to live under your mercy and in your love. Show me that way in Jesus. Amen.

"Christ's Spirit"

Read 1 Corinthians 2:16

Isaiah's question, "Is there anyone around who knows God's Spirit, anyone who knows what he is doing?" has been answered: Christ knows, and we have Christ's Spirit.

1 Corinthians 2:16

Having the mind of Christ means looking at things from God's side, thinking through things in order to implement redemption. It is a mind that we share when we accept God's rule and Christ's forgiveness and the Holy Spirit's gifts.

What scripture does Paul quote?

PRAYER: "Take Thou our minds, dear Lord, we humbly pray; Give us the mind of Christ each passing day; Teach us to know the truth that sets us free; Grant us in all our thoughts to honor Thee" (W. H. Foulkes, "Take Thou Our Minds, Dear Lord," The Hymnbook, 306). Amen.

"Acting Like Infants"
Read 1 Corinthians 3:1–4

> But for right now, friends, I'm completely
> frustrated by your unspiritual dealings
> with each other and with God. You're
> acting like infants in relation to Christ,
> capable of nothing much more than
> nursing at the breast.

> 1 Corinthians 3:1–2

Why do any of us take small items of spiritual
truth and use them to claim a superiority? As if
what I have or know makes me better than another! Don't I realize that the parts of the truth
that others have are just as important and essential
as those that I have?

What immaturities do you still hang on to?

PRAYER: Be patient, Lord, as you lead me through
my infancy into adulthood. Forgive me for the
childhood squabbles in which I, like a spoiled infant, try to get my own way. Make an adult out of
me, in Christ. *Amen.*

"God Made You Grow"
Read 1 Corinthians 3:5–8

I planted the seed, Apollos watered the
plants, but *God* made you grow.
1 Corinthians 3:6

No one person is most important; we are all given
important but yet minor parts. God is the central
figure and provides the essential energy. Our
efforts to see past persons and recognize God's
immediate presence must be incessant and unre-
lenting.

Who gets between you and God?

PRAYER: Lord, I want to appreciate what others do
in your name without idolizing them; I want to
be sensitive to every ministry but not let any be a
substitute for your presence in my life. In Jesus'
name. *Amen.*

MAY 20

"God's Field"

Read 1 Corinthians 3:9

> What makes them worth doing is the God
> we are serving. You happen to be God's
> field in which we are working.
>
> *1 Corinthians 3:9*

God is a farmer: each person is a plot of ground that is tilled, seeded, weeded, and harvested. God is a carpenter: each person is a building measured, sawed, and hammered together. These vivid images tell us that we receive ardent and skilled attention from God.

What is God doing in your life now?

PRAYER: I praise you, God, every time that I realize again how carefully and continuously your love comes to focus on me. Complete your design in who I am and what I do for the sake of Jesus Christ. *Amen.*

"Only One Foundation"
Read 1 Corinthians 3:10–11

Remember, there is only one foundation,
the one already laid: Jesus Christ.

1 Corinthians 3:11

There are numerous tasks in the Christian life and many ways of accomplishing them, but there is a single foundation. No one is permitted to go off and do his own thing. Always and everywhere we build on what God has shown and acted in Jesus Christ. We do not strive for originality but for faithfulness.

What is the purpose of a foundation?

PRAYER: Dear Lord, I do not want my life to be a series of makeshift shanties thrown together out of my impulses and desires. I want everything I live—my work, my conversation, my love—to be built on Christ, the sure foundation. Amen.

"Going to Be an Inspection"
Read 1 Corinthians 3:12–15

Eventually there is going to be an inspection. If you use cheap or inferior materials, you'll be found out.

1 Corinthians 3:13

It matters what we do. It makes a difference if we
work well or ill, if we live sincerely or hypocritically, if we live in love or indifference. Our actions
count and our faith counts. Everything in our lives
is significant.

What is the day of "inspection" Paul speaks of?

PRAYER: You show me, God, the essential dignity
of all my actions in faith: keep me on my toes,
aware that nothing is wasted when done in love
and that anything is valuable when done with
grace. Amen.

"You *Are* the Temple of God"
Read 1 Corinthians 3:16–17

You realize, don't you, that you are the
temple of God, and God himself is
present in you?

1 Corinthians 3:16

Our bodies are holy—set apart for sacred use. Our
bodies are where all love is expressed and forgiveness experienced and grace shared. The gospel insists on the importance of the physical. As we
mature in faith we do not become less "physical"
and more "spiritual"; rather, the spiritual intensifies and celebrates the physical.

How do you treat your "temple"?

PRAYER: Creator Christ, how many times have I
complained about this body because it doesn't appear or feel or respond the way I wish. Forgive me
for my ingratitude: it is your gift, your temple.
Fill it with glory and holiness. *Amen.*

"The Chicanery of the Chic"
Read 1 Corinthians 3:18–20

What the world calls smart, God calls
    stupid. It's written in Scripture,
    "He exposes the chicanery of the chic.
The Master sees through the smoke
      screens
of the know-it-alls."

1 Corinthians 3:19

The so-called wisdom that Paul warns about is a
cleverness that pretends to solve the meaning of
life apart from God, that thinks that intelligence
supersedes faith and that knowledge in itself produces goodness.

    Give an example of "chicanery."

PRAYER: God, you have given me a mind to use in
your service: I bring every thought captive to
your lordship; I submit my imagination to your
revelation; in the name and for the sake of Jesus.
Amen.

"Everything Is Already Yours"
Read 1 Corinthians 3:21–23

I don't want to hear any of you bragging
about yourself or anyone else. Everything is already yours as a gift.

1 Corinthians 3:21

Grasping for advantage is futile. Ambition motivated by jealousy is a waste. Competition driven
by envy is vanity. People of faith already have
everything that we need—in Christ.

What do you want that you do not need?

PRAYER: Thank you, dear Christ, for giving me life
and salvation and love. I want to experience the
deepest dimensions of what is already given. By
your grace I will do it and live in gratitude and
praise. *Amen.*

"Guides . . . , Not Security Guards"
Read 1 Corinthians 4:1

> Don't imagine us leaders to be something
> we aren't. We are servants of Christ, not
> his masters. We are guides into God's
> most sublime secrets, not security
> guards posted to protect them.
>
> 1 Corinthians 4:1

People who are given places of leadership in the church are not to be looked up to as if they had some special power, nor envied as if they had some special privilege, but simply accepted for the services they provide and the work they complete.

How do you treat those who are in positions of ministry?

PRAYER: God, I thank you for the servants and guides you have given me. I accept their work and appreciate their ministry. Help me to honor you, not by putting them on a pedestal, but by putting into faith and action the truth that they represent. *Amen.*

"Jump to Conclusions"
1 Corinthians 4:2–5

So don't get ahead of the Master and jump
to conclusions with your judgments
before all the evidence is in. When he
comes, he will bring out in the open
and place in evidence all kinds of things
we never even dreamed of—inner
motives and purposes and prayers. Only
then will any one of us get to hear the
"Well done!" of God.

1 Corinthians 4:5

The judgments that we make on one another are
always premature and based on insufficient evidence. Only God can see into our hearts, weigh
our motives, and evaluate our entire lives. Christians are not exempt from criticism, but we prefer
to submit to what God decides about us rather
than to what the crowd thinks.

What do you expect from God's judgment?

PRAYER: O Judge of all the earth, I live in anticipa-
tion of your judgment when you will sort out my
mixed motives, clarify my confused goals, and
complete what you have begun in Jesus Christ.
Amen.

"Pertain to Apollos and Me"
Read 1 Corinthians 4:6–7

All I'm doing right now, friends, is showing how these things pertain to Apollos
and me so that you will learn restraint
and not rush into making judgments
without knowing all the facts. It's important to look at things from God's point of
view. I would rather not see you inflating
or deflating reputations based on mere
hearsay.

1 Corinthians 4:6

Paul first lives out the basic truths in his own life
and then talks about them. He opens the pages of
scripture and also the doors of his own heart so
that others not only hear the truth but see the
process by which it is believed and incorporated
into a life of faith.

What truth are you applying to yourself today?

PRAYER: Before I ever think of telling anyone else
what to do, Lord, help me to thoroughly live it out
myself. Be with me as I learn firsthand the meaning of your commands and blessings. I want the
journal of this day to be a direct and honest narra-
tive of the same salvation story that is told in scripture. Amen.

MAY 29

"All You Need"
Read 1 Corinthians 4:8

You already have all you need. You already
have more access to God than you can
handle. Without bringing either Apollos
or me into it, you're sitting on top of the
world—at least God's world—and we're
right there, sitting alongside you!

1 Corinthians 4:8

The Christian task is not to get more—we already
have all we need!—but to share what we have; nor
to acquire power—we are already kings!—but to
share our strength. The gospel reverses old sin-
habits of getting more and sets up a counter-
movement of giving away.

Are you a "getter" or a "giver"?

PRAYER: Voices all around us, Lord, are urging me
to buy this and get that, to take over this and take
charge of that. Help me to go against the stream
and accept the abundance of what you have given
and then actively seek ways to share it. *Amen.*

"The Messiah's Misfits"
Read 1 Corinthians 4:9–13

> We're the Messiah's misfits. You might be
> sure of yourselves, but we live in the
> midst of frailties and uncertainties. You
> might be well-thought-of by others, but
> we're mostly kicked around.
>
> 1 Corinthians 4:10

Christians who want to justify a life of conspicuous consumption will get no help from scripture. Alongside the Corinthian practice of acquiring things, boasting of goodness, and making a show of wisdom, Paul sets the apostolic experience of being weak and despised and living as misfits.

How many contrasts does Paul list?

PRAYER: "Daily our lives would show Weakness made strong, Toilsome and gloomy ways Brightened with song; Some deeds of kindness done, Some souls by patience won, Dear Lord, to Thee, Dear Lord, to Thee" (Edwin P. Parker, "Master, No Offering Costly and Sweet," The Hymnbook, 299). Amen.

MAY 31

"Aren't Many Fathers"
Read 1 Corinthians 4:14–16

There are a lot of people around who
    can't wait to tell you what you've done
    wrong, but there aren't many fathers
    willing to take the time and effort to
    help you grow up. It was as Jesus helped
    me proclaim God's Message to you that
    I became your father.

1 Corinthians 4:15

Many people point us the way or tell us what to
do; a few people share their lives, suffer with us,
and patiently work through the stages of growth
in grace. Guides are not without their usefulness,
but "fathers" are invaluable.

Who has been a father (or mother) to you in
the faith?

PRAYER: I lift up to you in gratitude and praise
the people who have taught and trained and loved
me with your love, O Christ. Thank you for using
their faithfulness, their perseverance, and their affection to help me grow up in grace. *Amen.*

"My Dear Son"
Read 1 Corinthians 4:17

This is why I sent Timothy to you earlier.
He is also my dear son, and true to the
Master. He will refresh your memory on
the instructions I regularly give all the
churches on the way of Christ.

1 Corinthians 4:17

Where there are fathers in the family of Christ
there are also children. Timothy followed in the
footsteps of his faith-father in practicing the ministry of Christ. Thus leadership expanded and de-
veloped and prospered.

Read more about Timothy in Acts 16:1–5.

PRAYER: God, am I a "dear son (or daughter), and
true to the Master"? I want to be. I want to be en-
trusted with saying and acting in ways that bring
others into the family and help them to grow up
in Christ. *Amen.*

JUNE 2

"Not a Matter of Mere Talk"
Read 1 Corinthians 4:18–21

God's Way is not a matter of mere talk;
it's an empowered life.

1 Corinthians 4:20

Paul has a difficult pastoral task: to direct a confused Corinthian congregation through a crowded
marketplace of arrogant religious hucksters into
direct faith-participation with the person of Christ.
He has to get them past the distracting claims and
counterclaims of what is being said and sold in the
name of God to the place where they themselves
freely experience God in Christ.

Did Paul use the rod of love?

PRAYER: Everything you provide for me, Father,
seems designed to get me to accept, and praise and
follow; not speculate, or bargain, or talk. I want to
experience the powerful meanings of your rule in
Christ: by faith, and by your grace, I will. *Amen.*

"Doesn't Even Faze You!"
Read 1 Corinthians 5:1–2

And you're so above it all that it doesn't
   even faze you! Shouldn't this break your
   hearts? Shouldn't it bring you to your
   knees in tears? Shouldn't this person and
   his conduct be confronted and dealt
   with?

1 Corinthians 5:2

Being works itself out in behavior. But some, and
church history is full of examples, instead of becoming in action what they believe, arrogantly
paste their so-called beliefs on themselves like
labels, presuming to justify whatever they want
to do.

Do you behave the way you believe?

PRAYER: Lord, it is easy for me to see the wrongs
that other people do—their inconsistencies, their
misbehavior. It is difficult to see what I am doing.
I want my behavior to grow out of my belief, not
contradict it. Help me to do that in the name of
Jesus. Amen.

JUNE 4

"Forgiven Before the Master"
Read 1 Corinthians 5:3–5

Hold this man's conduct up to public
scrutiny. Let him defend it if he can!
But if he can't, then out with him! It
will be totally devastating to him, of
course, and embarrassing to you. But
better devastation and embarrassment
than damnation. You want him on his
feet and forgiven before the Master on
the Day of Judgment.

1 Corinthians 5:5

Paul combines harshness and mercy, severity and
compassion. He pronounces judgment in the expectation of salvation. The offensive sin is condemned outright, but the confused sinner is offered to God for salvation.

How does judgment contribute to salvation?

PRAYER: God, I want to have the mind of Paul in
this: to be full of indignation at sin and full of
compassion for the sinner. Give me the ability to
separate the two and to pray with like discern-
ment. Amen.

JUNE 5

"A 'Small Thing'"
Read 1 Corinthians 5:6–8

Your flip and callous arrogance in these
things bothers me. You pass it off as a
small thing, but it's anything but that.
Yeast, too, is a "small thing," but it
works its way through a whole batch
of bread dough pretty fast.

1 Corinthians 5:6

Yeast, in scripture, is often used to symbolize sin.
It takes only a little yeast to make itself felt
through the entire loaf of bread. Boasting is like
that. Any sin is like that. We cannot be too vigilant
in guarding against it and getting rid of it.

What does yeast have to do with the Passover
Lamb?

PRAYER: I live in a world, Lord, where sin is condoned and overlooked, rationalized and excused.
Few understand its power and destruction. Cleanse
me of it and protect me from it, in the strong
name of Jesus Christ. *Amen.*

"You Can't Just Go Along with This"
Read 1 Corinthians 5:9–11

But I am saying that you shouldn't act as
if everything is just fine when one of
your Christian companions is promis-
cuous or crooked, is flip with God or
rude to friends, gets drunk or becomes
greedy and predatory. You can't just go
along with this, treating it as acceptable
behavior.

1 Corinthians 5:11

Paul is authoritative in his distinction: we are to
mingle freely with the sinners in the world; we
are to be alert to sin in the community of faith. It
is part of our witness to accept sinners in the
world on their own terms; it is softheaded to con-
done hypocrisy among the faithful.

How do you make the distinction in your
everyday life?

PRAYER: Lord Jesus Christ, show me how to be
generous with and gracious to all those who are
in the world; and show me how to be firm with
all my brothers and sisters in faith; even as you ate
with prostitutes but drove money changers from
the temple. Amen.

"God Decides on the Outsiders"
Read 1 Corinthians 5:12–13

God decides on the outsiders, but we need
to decide when our brothers and sisters
are out of line and, if necessary, clean
house.

1 Corinthians 5:13

We have it exactly backwards. We rage in indignation against the murderers and rapists and bur-
glars that we read of in the newspapers; we make
every kind of excuse for those with whom we eat
friendly meals at church suppers.

How can you use this counsel?

PRAYER: I don't, Lord, make the same mistake so
often in my own family. I love and confront and,
when I can, correct them. Why don't I do it with
brothers and sisters in faith? Is it that I don't believe that they really are brothers and sisters? Or is
it that I simply don't care? *Amen.*

JUNE 8

"A Jury Made Up of Christians"
Read 1 Corinthians 6:1–6

The day is coming when the world is
going to stand before a jury made up
of Christians. If someday you are going
to rule on the world's fate, wouldn't it
be a good idea to practice on some of
these smaller cases?

1 Corinthians 6:2

When it comes to settling differences, secular law
courts are a very poor second to the Christian
faith community. Christians at worship are in a
place where confessions are made, forgiveness
learned, and justice understood firsthand, with
Christ himself as a merciful judge.

How do you settle legal differences?

PRAYER: "My theme song is God's love and justice,
and I'm singing it right to you, Yahweh. I'm finding my way down the road of right living, but
how long before you show up? I'm doing the very
best I can, and I'm doing it at home, where it
counts. I refuse to take a second look at corrupting
people and degrading things" (Psalm 101:1–3).
Amen.

JUNE 9

"Be Wronged and Forget It?"
Read 1 Corinthians 6:7–8

These court cases are an ugly blot on your
community. Wouldn't it be far better to
just take it, to let yourselves be wronged
and forget it?

1 Corinthians 6:7

Christians have different standards than those in
the world. The big question is not, How can I get
what is due to me? but, How can I experience and
express the grace of Christ?

Are you willing to subordinate law to grace?

PRAYER: Lord, I don't want to live one way in the
church and another way outside it. I want the way
of grace to inform my relationships and my decisions everywhere and with everyone. Lead me in
that way, in the name of Jesus. *Amen.*

"A Fresh Start"
Read 1 Corinthians 6:9–11

A number of you know from experience
what I'm talking about, for not so long
ago you were on that list. Since then,
you've been cleaned up and given a
fresh start by Jesus, our Master, our
Messiah, and by our God present in
us, the Spirit.

1 Corinthians 6:11

The Christian—but how frequently we need to be
told!—is shaped not by old sins but by new grace.
It is Christ's new gracious acts that make us what
we are, not our old sinful ones.

What does Christ think of you?

PRAYER: God, show me myself in the clear mirror
of your grace, not through the flawed and dis-
torted glass of my sins. Give me a good look at the
new creation that you have made me, so that I
may choose rightly and live freely. Amen.

"Just Because"
Read 1 Corinthians 6:12–14

Just because something is technically legal
   doesn't mean that it's spiritually appropriate. If I went around doing whatever
   I thought I could get by with, I'd be a
   slave to my whims.

                                 1 Corinthians 6:12

In the exhilaration of discovering that we are accepted by God regardless—that we live by grace
not by works—some throw caution to the winds
and live impulsively and lawlessly. But living in
Christ also means living *well*—wisely and skillfully. Christians are moral, not to escape wrath,
but to enjoy goodness.

   What are some things you have found to be
unhelpful?

PRAYER: I need a completely new way of asking
questions, O God: a change from the minimum,
asking what can I get by with, to the maximum,
asking what I can do that will allow me to live au-
thentically and to your glory. *Amen.*

JUNE 12

"The Sacredness of Our Own Bodies"
Read 1 Corinthians 6:15–18

There is a sense in which sexual sins are
   different from all others. In sexual sin
   we violate the sacredness of our own
   bodies, these bodies that were made
   for God-given and God-modeled love,
   for "becoming one" with another.
                              1 Corinthians 6:18

The body is important to the Christian, but not
for indulgence or pampering. Its genius is as a
means of expressing in specific times and places
and with actual people every aspect of the gospel.
Immorality is not wrong because it emphasizes
the physical but because it ignores the spiritual.

What moral dangers do you need to guard
against?

PRAYER: Lord Jesus Christ, develop my moral sense
so that I can avoid the deception all around me and
still live creatively and with initiative, using my
whole person—body and spirit—to your glory.
Amen.

"See God in and Through Your Body"
Read 1 Corinthians 6:19–20

The physical part of you is not some piece
of property belonging to the spiritual
part of you. God owns the whole works.
So let people see God in and through
your body.

1 Corinthians 6:20

Our bodies are to be used to express ourselves to
God and our neighbors—in faith and love. Bodies
are the means by which every spiritual reality ac-
quires physical expression.

Compare this with 1 Corinthians 3:16–17.

PRAYER: "So let our lips and lives express The holy
gospel we profess; So let our works and virtues
shine, To prove the doctrine all divine" (Isaac
Watts, "So Let Our Lips and Lives Express," *The
Hymnbook*, 289). *Amen.*

JUNE 14

"God Gives the Gift"
Read 1 Corinthians 7:1–7

Sometimes I wish everyone were single
like me—a simpler life in many ways!
But celibacy is not for everyone any
more than marriage is. God gives the
gift of the single life to some, the gift
of the married life to others.

1 Corinthians 7:7

Marriage is a gift of God; to be unmarried is also
a gift of God. Either condition has its special and
unique qualities to be explored and enjoyed in the
way of joyful faith.

What is your special gift?

PRAYER: God, I accept what you have given and
will give me. With the gift, provide wisdom to
use it as a means of sharing your grace and loving
you. Let me not be envious of what I do not have
or proud of what I do have. *Amen.*

"Tell the Unmarried"
Read 1 Corinthians 7:8–9

I do, though, tell the unmarried and
widows that singleness might well be
the best thing for them, as it has been
for me.

1 Corinthians 7:8

To be unmarried is not a disaster, is not a sign of
inadequacy, and is not to be considered something less than the best. Paul discovered in the single life ways to love that were inaccessible to the
married. To be single is neither unnatural nor un-
desirable.

How do you look on the single life?

PRAYER: Father, I don't want propaganda or senti-
ment to shape my expectations of the complete
life. I want to discover my true being in relation to
you. Show me my unique gifts and the goals that
you provide for me in Jesus Christ. *Amen.*

"If You Are Married"
Read 1 Corinthians 7:10–11

And if you are married, stay married.
 This is the Master's command, not mine.
                                    1 Corinthians 7:10

To be married is not a disaster and is not to be considered an imprisonment. Paul viewed marriage not primarily as a way of arriving at happiness, but as a way of realizing the disciplines of love.

Read Paul's statement on marriage in Ephesians 5:21–33.

PRAYER: God, I'm always asking what will make me happy; teach me instead to discover what will make me whole. Stretch and strengthen me to live up and into your righteousness, not down to the level of my selfishness. *Amen.*

JUNE 17

"As Peacefully as We Can"
Read 1 Corinthians 7:12–16

On the other hand, if the unbelieving
spouse walks out, you've got to let him
or her go. You don't have to hold on
desperately. God has called us to make
the best of it, as peacefully as we can.

1 Corinthians 7:15

The task is not to reform the unbelieving partner
nor to avoid him or her, but to believe in Christ
and accept the partner. The Christian insight is
that faith is more powerful than unbelief and that
quiet acceptance is victorious over unbelieving rejection.

Whom do you need to accept?

PRAYER: I am always looking for a quick solution,
Lord, when you are urging me into a lifetime of
discipleship. I want to fix the people around me
while you are offering to change *me* into your likeness. Let your redemptive peace overcome my impatient meddling. *Amen.*

JUNE 18

"Paid Out for Your Ransom"
Read 1 Corinthians 7:17–24

Then a huge sum was paid out for your
ransom. So please don't, out of old
habit, slip back into being or doing
what everyone else tells you.

1 Corinthians 7:23

We do not change by changing roles but by being
changed by Christ. At immense cost, each person
has been redefined and set free for a life of faith:
we simply must not submit to the tyranny of the
world's mislabeling.

What unsatisfactory labels do people put on
you?

PRAYER: How difficult I find it, dear God, to escape
the imprisoning expectations of my friends and
family—of myself! Yet you have set me free from
them, I know, at the cross. Help me to live out my
new being, right where I am, by the power of your
Holy Spirit. Amen.

"On Its Way Out"
Read 1 Corinthians 7:25–31

This world as you see it is on its way out.
1 Corinthians 7:31b

The insight that "this world as you see it is on its way out" is as true now as it was in the first century. The life of faith penetrates to the inside of things so that we do not waste attention or energy on what is merely fashionable.

Why does Paul distinguish "direction" from "counsel"?

PRAYER: Lord Jesus Christ, when I try to change my circumstances to fit my desires, show me how to find your presence and the working out of your will in the center of where I am right now. *Amen.*

"Without a Lot of Distractions"
Read 1 Corinthians 7:32–35

I'm trying to be helpful and make it as easy
as possible for you, not make things
harder. All I want is for you to be able to
develop a way of life in which you can
spend plenty of time together with the
Master without a lot of distractions.

1 Corinthians 7:35

Paul's genius is that he never gets distracted from
the central reality: our relation to the Lord. Everything is evaluated in terms of how it encourages
or discourages our love for and faith in Christ. He
has no other standard, no other interest.

What distracts you from spending "plenty of
time together with the Master"?

PRAYER: Give me, God, the single eye and the
united heart. Take all my feelings and tasks and
experiences and thoughts and weave them into a
single strand of devotion to you, in Jesus Christ.
Amen.

"Pastoral Reasons"
Read 1 Corinthians 7:36–38

Marriage is spiritually and morally right
and not inferior to singleness in any
way, although as I indicated earlier,
because of the times we live in, I do
have pastoral reasons for encouraging
singleness.

1 Corinthians 7:38

Paul does not dictate a single, rigid, perfectionist rule. He permits variations in response according to each person's circumstances and abilities. He wisely knows that many decisions are not between right and wrong but between the appropriate and the possible. And so he encourages the good, the better, and the best in us, at whatever our stage of readiness and growth.

What issue is Paul dealing with?

PRAYER: I appreciate counselors like Paul, Lord, who do not force every question into categories of black and white but allow me the freedom to grow from what I am to what I can be by your grace. *Amen.*

"The Blessing of the Master"
Read 1 Corinthians 7:39–40

A wife must stay with her husband as
   long as he lives. If he dies, she is free
   to marry anyone she chooses. She will,
   of course, want to marry a believer and
   have the blessing of the Master.

                                   1 Corinthians 7:39

There is far more variety in the life of faith than in
the life of unbelief. Devotion to Christ has many
more sides to it and dimensions in it than does
headstrong rebellion. "Marrying a believer and
having the blessing of the Master" is a commitment that opens doors to freedom. Once we step
out of that commitment, we return to narrow ruts
of habit or anxiety or doubt.

How has your freedom expanded in "having
the blessing of the Master"?

PRAYER: God, never let me wander from the cross
of Christ where I first experienced my freedom.
Never, in the thrill of choosing my way, let me
forget that I have been chosen. Never, in the liberty of being set in a broad place, let me forget
that it is the place of faith. *Amen.*

"Humble Hearts"

Read 1 Corinthians 8:1–3

We sometimes tend to think we know all
we need to know to answer these kinds
of questions—but sometimes our humble
hearts can help us more than our proud
minds.

1 Corinthians 8:2

Some items of Christian lifestyle change from generation to generation. A first-century question that we no longer deal with was, "Should we eat food offered to idols?" Paul was more interested in how the Christians responded than in what they answered: would they use the question to exercise personal love or to assert superior knowledge?

What lifestyle questions do you face?

PRAYER: As I work out in word and deed my life in your service, help me, Lord, to be motivated most of all by how I have been known by you, not by what I know about you, so that others are built up by my love for them, not put down by my display of knowledge. *Amen.*

JUNE 24

"No God Other Than Our One God"
Read 1 Corinthians 8:4–6

Some people say, quite rightly, that idols
have no actual existence, that there's
nothing to them, that there is no God
other than our one God, that no matter
how many of these so-called gods are
named and worshiped they still don't
add up to anything but a tall story.

1 Corinthians 8:4

In the process of being sensitive to the scruples
and sensitivities of others, we must not adopt their
superstitions as our own. When the early Christians avoided food offered to idols, it was not because they supposed the idols had contaminated
the food, but because they did not want their actions misinterpreted as an act of worship of idols.

Summarize Paul's reasoning here.

PRAYER: Almighty God, keep my thinking straight
while I am developing sympathies. I want to do
the right things, but I also want to do them for the
right reasons, in the name of and always for the
sake of Jesus Christ. Amen.

JUNE 25

"Thrown Off Track"
Read 1 Corinthians 8:7–13

But God *does* care when you use your
freedom carelessly in a way that leads a
Christian still vulnerable to those old
associations to be thrown off track.

1 Corinthians 8:9

Freedom in Christ is not a license to do what we
wish, but a liberty to be creative and innovative in
expressing love and sharing joy, smoothing the
way to faith for those who are frightened or be-
wildered.

Who among your friends is "still vulnerable"?

PRAYER: At the same time, O God, that you are
creating in me a new openness to your word and
will, develop my sensitivities to the feelings of
those around me so that to them my life may be
an invitation, not a stumbling block, to goodness.
Amen.

JUNE 26

"I'm Perfectly Free"
Read 1 Corinthians 9:1–2

And don't tell me that I have no authority
to write like this. I'm perfectly free to
do this—isn't that obvious? Haven't I
been given a job to do? Wasn't I com-
missioned to this work in a face-to-face
meeting with Jesus, our Master? Aren't
you yourselves proof of the good work
that I've done for the Master?

1 Corinthians 9:1

The best way to get at the meaning of freedom in
Christ is not to go to a dictionary for the definition
of the word, but to look at a living instance of it.
Paul offers himself as such an instance: he is ever
experiencing new dimensions of freedom in the
life in Christ that he is practicing and preaching.

What is attractive to you in Paul's freedom?

PRAYER: It is your word, Christ, that makes me
free; not my rebellion against authority or my de-
fiance of convention. Free me from narrowness
and from selfishness so that others may also find
freedom in my company. *Amen.*

"Authority of My Commission"
Read 1 Corinthians 9:3–7

> Even if no one else admits the authority of
> my commission, you can't deny it. Why,
> my work with you is living proof of my
> authority!
>
> 1 Corinthians 9:3

Paul was out to serve the Lord, not carry out some assigned functions that would please religious consumers. Because he didn't fit into what others thought he ought to be, he was roundly criticized.

What exactly, do you think, was Paul criticized for?

PRAYER: Lord Jesus Christ, you have not only set me free, you have also set others free. Even as I enjoy my own freedom, help me to celebrate the freedom of others, not trying to squeeze them into my idea of what I think they should do, but releasing them for what you lead them to be. Amen.

JUNE 28

"Expecting Something"
Read 1 Corinthians 9:8–11

Don't you think his concern extends to
us? Of course. Farmers plow and thresh
expecting something when the crop
comes in.

1 Corinthians 9:10

We live in a world in which money and food and
clothing are quite as real as prayer and praise and
preaching. Christians do not become less concerned with the former as they become practiced
in the latter. The gospel is a discovery of the *inner-
connectedness*, not the separation, of visible and invisible, of heaven and earth.

What do you get out of being a Christian?

PRAYER: Father, don't let me fool myself into thinking that my concern for things spiritual excuses
me from responsibilities in things material. As I
become more "heavenly minded," help me to become more "earthly good." *Amen.*

"Rather Than to Get in the Way"
Read 1 Corinthians 9:12–14

> Others demand plenty from you in
> these ways. Don't we who have never
> demanded deserve even more? But
> we're not going to start demanding
> now what we've always had a perfect
> right to. Our decision all along has
> been to put up with anything rather
> than to get in the way or detract from
> the Message of Christ.
>
> 1 Corinthians 9:12

To the stingy and niggardly, who are unwilling to support pastoral work in the church, Paul insists that a congregation must provide adequately for such ministry. But he does not insist on his own rights in this regard lest he be suspected of using scripture to line his own pockets.

What scripture does Paul use to support his argument?

PRAYER: Merciful and gracious Father, when I meet people who are generous, help me not to take advantage of them, seeing just another chance to get something for nothing. Use them to excite a similar generosity in me. *Amen.*

"Compelled to Do It"
Read 1 Corinthians 9:15–18

If I proclaim the Message, it's not to get
something out of it for myself. I'm
compelled to do it, and doomed if I don't!

1 Corinthians 9:16

Paul's motivation for telling people that God loves
them in Christ is not money but mercy: he is in-
wardly compelled by his deep immersion in forgiveness and grace. True ministry is a way of giving, not of getting.

What motivates you?

PRAYER: "All things are Thine; no gift have we,
Lord of all gifts, to offer Thee; And hence with
grateful hearts today Thine own before Thy feet
we lay" (John Greenleaf Whittier, "All Things Are
Thine," *The Hymnbook*, 555). *Amen.*

JULY 1

"Every Sort of Servant"
Read 1 Corinthians 9:19–23

I kept my bearings in Christ—but I entered
their world and tried to experience things
from their point of view. I've become
just about every sort of servant there is
in my attempts to lead those I meet into
a God-saved life.

1 Corinthians 9:22

Paul cared little for what people thought of him.
His secure inner identity gave him great freedom
to be creative in his witness to others. Confidence
at the center provided flexibility at the circumference.

What is the difference between *flexible* and *un-
principled*?

PRAYER: Free me, Christ, from the legislation of
public opinion and the tyranny of peer pressure
so that I may live freely and imaginatively, every
day finding fresh and convincing ways to tell people who do not know you that you are Lord and
Savior. *Amen.*

JULY 2

"Hard for the Finish Line"
Read 1 Corinthians 9:24–27

I don't know about you, but I'm running
hard for the finish line. I'm giving it
everything I've got.

1 Corinthians 9:26

Some people, when they lose their sense of direction, increase their activity. But no amount of religious bustle can compensate for the absence of a goal. For the Christian, as for the athlete, a focused purpose eliminates "running around" and replaces it with running *to*.

What is the goal?

PRAYER: "'Tis God's all animating voice That calls thee from on high; 'Tis His own hand presents the prize To thine aspiring eye. Blest Saviour, introduced by Thee, Have I my race begun; And, crowned with victory, at Thy feet I'll lay my honors down" (Philip Doddridge, "Awake, My Soul, Stretch Every Nerve," *The Hymnbook*, 346). *Amen.*

"They All Ate and Drank"

Read 1 Corinthians 10:1–5

They all ate and drank identical food and
drink, meals provided daily by God.
They drank from the Rock, God's fountain for them that stayed with them
wherever they were. And the Rock was
Christ.

1 Corinthians 10:3–4

Consumerism in the church is abhorrent. It is also
common: people rush to get spiritual blessings at
bargain prices in order to look better or feel hap-
pier. But it didn't work in Israel and it won't work
with us. God does not want consumers, but cre-
ators-believers who share the Spirit's work of shaping a life to the glory of God.

What "sea" does Paul refer to?

PRAYER: Great God, I want to respond to what I
see in praise and faith and obedience, accepting
what you give in order to be the person you call
into being in and through Jesus Christ. *Amen.*

JULY 4

"Be on Guard"
Read 1 Corinthians 10:6–10

> The same thing could happen to us. We
> must be on guard so that we never get
> caught up in wanting our own way as
> they did.
>
> 1 Corinthians 10:6

It is not necessary for each person to reenact every
sin. If we pay attention to our ancestors in the
faith, we can skip repeating their mistakes. Only
those who ignore history are condemned to repeat it.

What three typical sins are remembered here?

PRAYER: Thank you, Lord, for the clearly marked
map of Israel's faith journey. Train me to read it
well, so that I stay on the road of truth and life and
off the detours of idolatry and immorality and
pride. *Amen.*

JULY 5

"Could Fall Flat"
Read 1 Corinthians 10:11–12

You're not exempt. You could fall flat
   on your face as easily as anyone else.
   Forget about self-confidence; it's
   useless. Cultivate God-confidence.
1 Corinthians 10:12

Every impulse to do it on our own is a potential hazard to our progress in faith. For no one develops a mature relationship with God except by exercising trust and demonstrating dependence in ever new and more numerous ways.

What is the difference between assurance and overconfidence?

PRAYER: I don't want to become more independent, but more dependent, Lord. I want to find more ways to receive your help, to experience your providence, to accept your mercy and grace. I want you involved in every detail of my life, even as you have promised by your Holy Spirit. *Amen.*

JULY 6

"Help You Come Through It"
Read 1 Corinthians 10:13

No test or temptation that comes your way
is beyond the course of what others have
had to face. All you need to remember is
that God will never let you down; he'll
never let you be pushed past your limit;
he'll always be there to help you come
through it.

1 Corinthians 10:13

Every temptation has a way out. Nothing that we
encounter or experience is able, in itself, to defeat
us. And not only is there a way out, there is a map
of the way out—similar temptations have been
met by people of faith. Scripture tells the stories
of how our faithful God always provides strength
and wisdom for survival.

What temptation seems overpowering to you?

PRAYER: God, I know your promises and I know
the stories of the people who have experienced
your promises. When "the lust of the flesh and
the lust of the eyes and the pride of life" (1 John
2:16) or the cares of this world threaten to entrap
me, show me the way out, in Jesus' name. *Amen.*

"Reducing God"
Read 1 Corinthians 10:14–17

So, my very dear friends, when you see
people reducing God to something they
can use or control, get out of their
company as fast as you can.

1 Corinthians 10:14

Christians do not grow by stuffing ourselves with religious food regardless of its origin. Christ is our complete meal; therefore, we must not "eat" or "drink" anything else lest we ruin our digestive systems and spoil our appetites.

What do you need to say no to?

PRAYER: I come to you, Lord Jesus Christ, to get all that you give: I get everything I need—blessing and forgiveness, fellowship and love. As I receive your life by faith, make me into what you are so that I may live this day with energy and in celebration to the glory of God. *Amen.*

JULY 8

"Won't Put Up with It"
Read 1 Corinthians 10:18–22

> Besides, the Master won't put up with it.
> He wants us—all or nothing. Do you
> think you can get off with anything else?
> 1 Corinthians 10:22

We cannot, either logically or emotionally, live two religions: faith in Christ is all-involving. The God who created us entire redeems us completely. He won't have us in segments, or by fractions.

What were the Corinthians trying to do?

PRAYER: Lord, gather the scattered pieces of my imagination into a single vision of your salvation. Pull together all the vagrant impulses I have for goodness into a single act of devotion as I offer myself, soul and body, a living sacrifice. Amen.

"Not to Just Get By"
Read 1 Corinthians 10:23–24

Look at it one way, you could say, "Anything goes. Because of God's immense generosity and grace, we don't have to dissect and scrutinize every action to see if it will pass muster." But the point is not to just get by.

1 Corinthians 10:23

The new Christian attitude is: Now that I am free from having to please God and free from having to meet society's expectations, I am free to be creative and compassionate in worship and witness. In that freedom, what words and actions will best express God's love and mercy to the people I will meet this day?

How do you use your freedom on behalf of your neighbors?

PRAYER: Now, Lord, that I no longer have to be anxious about what you think about me, and no longer have to worry about what others think about me, show me how to use my inner freedom in being helpful to my friends and building up my neighbors, sharing your goodness with them in Jesus' name. *Amen.*

JULY 10

"The Earth . . . Is God's"
Read 1 Corinthians 10:25–26

"The earth," after all, "is God's, and
everything in it."

1 Corinthians 10:26

The meat market in Corinth posed a moral problem for Christians. Some of the meat on sale each day had been earlier offered in sacrifice to a pagan god. Was it a sin to buy such meat? No, wrote Paul. A worthless idol can't pollute a good piece of meat. Go ahead and buy whatever you can afford and will enjoy.

What psalm does Paul quote?

PRAYER: Thank you, God, for giving me leeway to enjoy and celebrate your diverse and rich creation. Thank you for spacious living—within and without—the height and depth and length and breadth of grace in Jesus Christ. *Amen.*

"Small-Minded People"
Read 1 Corinthians 10:27–30

> But, except for these special cases, I'm
> not going to walk around on eggshells
> worrying about what small-minded
> people might say; I'm going to stride
> free and easy, knowing what our large-
> minded Master has already said.
>
> 1 Corinthians 10:29

Paul counsels courtesy and concern—our free-dom in Christ must never be an occasion for scandal or offense. But he does not ask us to submit our conscience to the censorious nit-picking of a neurotic—Christ, after all, did set us free.

Give an instance of a "small-minded person."

PRAYER: God, I don't want to become nervous and timid, always worried over the disapproval of others. But neither do I want my carefreeness to be misunderstood as carelessness. Direct me in the middle way, in the name of Jesus the Way. *Amen.*

"Do Everything That Way"

Read 1 Corinthians 10:31

So eat your meals heartily, not worrying
about what others say about you—
you're eating to God's glory, after all,
not to please them. As a matter of fact,
do everything that way, heartily and
freely to God's glory.

1 Corinthians 10:31

All behavior, in one way or another, is witness—
an unfurling of the banners of God's good news
of triumph and grace. Whatever puts that on display is the right action and the apt word for ex-
hibiting an aspect of glory.

What besides eating and drinking is a mode of
witness?

PRAYER: Lord, show me how to be innovative and
inventive by using the stuff of my everyday life
to make visible to others the world you made in
beauty and the life you redeem for salvation. *Amen.*

"I Hope You Will Be, Too"
Read 1 Corinthians 10:32–11:1

I try my best to be considerate of everyone's feelings in all these matters; I hope
you will be, too.

1 Corinthians 10:33

Paul invites his Corinthian friends to join him in
the exacting and glorious life of following in
Christ's way. He does not arrogantly stand above
them and lecture, nor does he in false humility
put himself beneath them and encourage them to
live better than he is willing to venture himself.

Are you willing to share your life like this?

PRAYER: I give you thanks, Lord, for companions
on the way, the people who share their ventures
and struggles with me, their hopes and fears, their
weaknesses and strengths. How much easier when
I have them to pray with, to talk things over with,
to work with! *Amen.*

"Keeping Up the Traditions"
Read 1 Corinthians 11:2

It pleases me that you continue to remember and honor me by keeping up the traditions of the faith I taught you. All actual authority stems from Christ.

1 Corinthians 11:2

While we do have to experience truth personally in the life of faith, we do not have to discover it by trial and error: there are well-marked paths (traditions) on which Christians may run in the race of faith.

What are some traditions that you appreciate?

PRAYER: What a rich heritage I have, God! I thank you for the truth-conserving stories and morals and customs that save me the trouble of personally testing out every religious suggestion for happiness and sampling every promised solution to sin. *Amen.*

"The Authority"

Read 1 Corinthians 11:3

In a marriage relationship, there is authority from Christ to husband, and from
husband to wife. The authority of Christ
is the authority of God.

1 Corinthians 11:3

God is to Christ as Christ is to man as man is to
woman. The comparisons are set side by side to
show that "authority" can hardly mean "boss," but
rather the one who loves and gives, saves and helps.
What is the relation of God to Christ?

PRAYER: O God, whenever I find myself in a
stronger position than the person next to me,
show me how to use that strength courteously
and mercifully, even as my Lord uses his strength
in me. *Amen.*

"Speaks with God or About God"
Read 1 Corinthians 11:4–10

Any man who speaks with God or about
   God in a way that shows a lack of respect
   for the authority of Christ, dishonors
   Christ. In the same way, a wife who
   speaks with God in a way that shows a
   lack of respect for the authority of her
   husband, dishonors her husband. Worse,
   she dishonors herself—an ugly sight,
   like a woman with her head shaved.
                          1 Corinthians 11:4–5

Praying and prophesying are forms of speech in
which we speak to God and for God. They must
not be engaged in casually or carelessly. Our appearance and dress must not be allowed to detract
from what we say.

   What would be an inappropriate dress or hairstyle for you?

PRAYER: Give me the sensitivity and good sense,
Father, to act and dress appropriately so that I do
not call attention to myself when I should be directing attention to you, for the sake of Jesus Christ.
Amen.

"Don't, by the Way"
Read 1 Corinthians 11:11–12

Don't, by the way, read too much into
  the differences here between men and
  women. Neither man nor woman can
  go it alone or claim priority. Man was
  created first, as a beautiful shining
  reflection of God—that is true. But
  the head on a woman's body clearly
  outshines in beauty the head of her
  "head," her husband. The first woman
  came from man, true—but ever since
  then, every man comes from a woman!
  And since virtually everything comes
  from God anyway, let's quit going
  through these "who's first" routines.

1 Corinthians 11:11–12

Our basic identities are not learned from the bio-
logical facts of sexuality but from the revealed
truths—"in the Lord." We discover who we are in
relation to others not competitively but coopera-
tively, not independently but dependently.

Rephrase Paul's argument.

PRAYER: God, as I live with people who are different from me in appearance and ability, use their
lives to complete some of my inadequacies and to
complement some of my shortcomings. *Amen.*

"Argumentative"
Read 1 Corinthians 11:13–16

I hope you're not going to be argumen-
tative about this. All God's churches see
it this way; I don't want you standing
out as an exception.

1 Corinthians 11:16

Not infrequently there are people who use the
church as a forum for asserting their own way.
They are more interested in arguing a point than
in attending to God's word. The church's unity is
restored when such people learn to submit themselves to God's will instead of parading their own
idiosyncrasies.

What is the cure for contention?

PRAYER: Use me, God, as a peacemaker. Give me
skills in breaking down differences, in finding
common grounds for worship and work, and in
dissolving the obstructions that impede the free
flow of your grace through my brothers and sisters in faith. *Amen.*

JULY 19

"Brings Out Your Worst Side"
Read 1 Corinthians 11:17–19

Regarding this next item, I'm not at all
pleased. I am getting the picture that
when you meet together it brings out
your worst side instead of your best!

1 Corinthians 11:17

Each gathering for worship in the name of God
must be a time of submission and listening, for
offering ourselves to God, not harnessing God to
the wagons of our egos. Otherwise, it brings out
the worst in us, not the best.

What happened in Corinth?

PRAYER: "I bow my forehead to the dust, I veil
mine eyes for shame, And urge, in trembling self-
distrust, A prayer without a claim. No offering of
mine own I have, No works my faith to prove; I can
but give the gifts He gave, And plead His love for
love" (John Greenleaf Whittier, "I Bow My Forehead to the Dust," The Hymnbook, 109). Amen.

"I Can't Believe It!"

Read 1 Corinthians 11:20–22

> I can't believe it! Don't you have your own
> homes to eat and drink in? Why would
> you stoop to desecrating God's church?
> Why would you actually shame God's
> poor? I never would have believed you
> would stoop to this. And I'm not going
> to stand by and say nothing.

1 Corinthians 11:22

The Lord's Table is the place where we begin to learn that there is always enough to go around when we offer ourselves in repentance and receive from our Lord in faith. It was a shock to Paul to find that in Corinth certain gluttons came to the Table to stuff themselves, and hungry people were turned away.

How do you express your concern for the hungry?

PRAYER: Am I this way, Lord? Am I more interested in getting my demands met than in receiving what you give and sharing it with others? Convert my demands into offerings and my greed into gratitude by the power of your Holy Spirit. *Amen.*

"Do This to Remember Me"
Read 1 Corinthians 11:23–26

Having given thanks, he broke it and said,
  "This is my body, broken for you. Do
  this to remember me."

1 Corinthians 11:24

All that God did in Christ to give us new life, all
that we receive from him to live the new life of
faith, is set forth clearly and simply and unforget-
tably in the Lord's Supper.

Why is the Lord's Supper important to you?

PRAYER: "For the bread, which Thou hast broken;
For the wine, which Thou hast poured; For the
words, which Thou hast spoken; Now we give
Thee thanks, O Lord" (Louis F. Benson, "For the
Bread, Which Thou Hast Broken," *The Hymnbook*,
449). *Amen.*

JULY 22

"Examine Your Motives"
Read 1 Corinthians 11:27–32

Examine your motives, test your heart,
come to this meal in holy awe.

1 Corinthians 11:28

Our self-examination is not to see if we are sinners, but to see if we are sincere. Do we come to
the Table to be made into what God wills for us in
Christ? Or do we come thoughtlessly and carelessly, assuming that "a little religion" might not
be a bad idea?

What does it mean to give "no thought about
the broken body of the Master"?

PRAYER: "Investigate my life, O God, find out
everything about me; Cross-examine and test me,
get a clear picture of what I'm about; See for
yourself whether I've done anything wrong—
then guide me on the road to eternal life" (Psalm
139:23–24). Amen.

JULY 23

"Be Reverent and Courteous"
Read 1 Corinthians 11:33–34

So, my friends, when you come together
to the Lord's Table, be reverent and
courteous with one another.
                                    1 Corinthians 11:33

The church is not a bonanza to which we greedily elbow our way to satisfy our lust for more. It is not where we come to get things at all, but where we meet persons—and are met by the person Jesus Christ.

What important persons do you meet in church?

PRAYER: Lord Jesus Christ, when I meet with your people, create in me the quietness out of which I can hear them speak; train me in the courtesies that convincingly demonstrate your grace. *Amen.*

"God's Spirit"
Read 1 Corinthians 12:1–3

What I want to talk about now is the
   various ways God's Spirit gets worked
   Into our lives. This is complex and often
   misunderstood, but I want you to be
   informed and knowledgeable.
                                    1 Corinthians 12:1

Just because something is spiritual, or even supernatural, does not mean that it is authentic. We
need instruction in distinguishing the genuine
from the counterfeit in things spiritual as well as
in things material.

At what point does Paul begin his instruction?

PRAYER: You have revealed yourself to me, O God,
in the person of Jesus Christ: instruct me thoroughly in his words and ways so that I will not be
easily taken in by attractive falsehoods. *Amen.*

"God's Various Gifts"
Read 1 Corinthians 12:4–7

God's various gifts are handed out
  everywhere; but they all originate
  in God's Spirit.

1 Corinthians 12:4

Different people experience different aspects of
God. But our differences in experience must never
be used to divide God into "gods." The pagan
Greeks had done that and the result was a mess.
God is one.

What was happening in Corinth?

PRAYER: God, there is too much majesty, too much
glory, too much blessing; my poor imagination
can't take it all in. Forgive me when I try to reduce
you to the size of my experience; keep me open
to the dimensions of your bounty, so that even
though I can't comprehend it all, I can praise you
always. *Amen.*

"He Decides"
Read 1 Corinthians 12:8–11

All these gifts have a common origin,
    but are handed out one by one by the
    one Spirit of God. He decides who gets
    what, and when.

1 Corinthians 12:11

Everyone gets something; no one gets everything. When I know that what I get is not an accident but God's considered choice for me, then I can be both grateful for what I receive and celebrative over the gifts received by others.

What gifts in others do you celebrate?

PRAYER: Thank you, Lord, for your gifts—the gifts that my friends get and the gifts that I get. Let me never be proud of what I have nor envious of what others have, but simply appreciative of your generosity. *Amen.*

"When We Were Baptized"
Read 1 Corinthians 12:12–13

By means of his one Spirit, we all said
goodbye to our partial and piecemeal
lives. We each used to independently call
our own shots, but then we entered into
a large and integrated life in which *he*
has the final say in everything. (This is
what we proclaimed in word and action
when we were baptized.)

1 Corinthians 12:13

Baptism signals a new identity: we are no longer
defined by race (Jew or Greek); we are no longer
defined by politics or economics (slave or free);
we are defined as persons raised to new life in
Christ.

Compare this with Romans 6:4.

PRAYER: God, it's hard to get rid of the old ways of
understanding myself. Sometimes I think that I
am better than others; sometimes I am convinced
that I am worse than others; and you tell me that
I am the *same* as others—neither better nor worse
but *redeemed*. Thank you. *Amen.*

JULY 28

"A Body"
Read 1 Corinthians 12:14

> I want you to think about how all this
> makes you more significant, not less.
> A body isn't just a single part blown
> up into something huge. It's all the
> different-but-similar parts arranged
> and functioning together.
>
> 1 Corinthians 12:14

Paul compares the community of people who believe in Christ to the human body—a complex, living organism with an incredible variety of parts, and no part unnecessary. It is one of his best images: once we grasp this way of looking at the church, a vast amount of misunderstanding is cleared up immediately.

How is your body like the church body?

PRAYER: Lord, help me to comprehend the many-leveled meanings of being a member of the body of Christ—all the aspects of interdependence, of organic life, of variety in appearance and function that you create in the church. *Amen.*

"Carefully Placed"
Read 1 Corinthians 12:15–21

As it is, we see that God has carefully
placed each part of the body right
where he wanted it.

1 Corinthians 12:18

The illustration is a cartoon: first a foot, then an
eye, and then an ear pretend to be the body. We
laugh. "You think that is comical?" says Paul, "but
it is exactly the way you appear when you pretend
to be superior to or separate from other Christians."

Do you ever do this?

PRAYER: Where am I in this arrangement, Lord?
What can I contribute and what do I need to receive? Show me my place and the place of all the
others in this marvelous arrangement that is your
church. *Amen.*

"A Model"
Read 1 Corinthians 12:22–25

The way God designed our bodies is a
model for understanding our lives
together as a church: every part dependent on every other part, the parts we
mention and the parts we don't, the
parts we see and the parts we don't.
1 Corinthians 12:24–25

It is obvious that in the body visible parts are not
more important than invisible parts. The hidden
parts of the body are as essential as the evident
parts. The obscure need not envy the prominent;
nor may the prominent look down on the obscure.

Are you a more or less hidden member?

PRAYER: Instead of seeking my place in the sun, I
want you to guide me, O God, in discovering your
place for me in the church, the place where I can
function in harmony with all whom you are using
to make your good news known and your grace
real. *Amen.*

"Involved in the Hurt"

Read 1 Corinthians 12:26

If one part hurts, every other part is
    involved in the hurt, and in the healing.
    If one part flourishes, every other part
    enters into the exuberance.

1 Corinthians 12:26

Sin separates us from God and from one another; salvation brings us together with God and each other. We cannot go off on our own, loving God by ourselves in our way; God in Christ has put us into a community where we experience the reality of the other.

Whose joy do you share? Whose pain?

PRAYER: I praise you, Almighty God, that I have not been turned loose to love and believe and hope alone, but that you have given me partners to share my joy and participate in my pain, even as Christ does. *Amen.*

"A Complete Body"
Read 1 Corinthians 12:27–30

> But it's obvious by now, isn't it, that Christ's
> church is a complete Body and not a
> gigantic, unidimensional Part?
>
> 1 Corinthians 12:27

We experience two fixed realities in the church:
we are all the same (a complete Body); we are all
different (not a unidimensional Part). Our unity
and our diversity both originate in God's appointment. Both realities must be embraced heartily
and lived gratefully.

How many items are in Paul's list?

PRAYER: As you lead me, God, to understand my
special gifts, help me at the same time to understand what I share with everyone. Keep me in
touch with what I have in common with all your
people and alive to the particular appointment
that you set for me. Amen.

"A Far Better Way"
Read 1 Corinthians 12:31

But now I want to lay out a far better way
for you.

1 Corinthians 12:31

The Christian's desires are to be directed to the
specific gifts that God has announced that he provides. The alternative is to have our inner lives debased by vagrant wishes—whims and impulses
left to the mercy of the world's stimuli.

What gifts do you desire?

PRAYER: "Come, Holy Ghost, our souls inspire,
And lighten with celestial fire; Thou the anointing
Spirit art, Who dost Thy seven-fold gifts impart.
Praise to Thy eternal merit, Father, Son, and Holy
Spirit" (old Latin hymn). *Amen.*

AUGUST 3

"The Creaking of a Rusty Gate"
Read 1 Corinthians 13:1

If I speak with human eloquence and
angelic ecstasy but don't love, I'm
nothing but the creaking of a rusty
gate.

1 Corinthians 13:1

All gifts and abilities are servants of love. When
they are not, they are debased into ugly parodies.
The most beautiful words, apart from love, are a
rude and grating assault on the ears.

What is "angelic ecstasy"?

PRAYER: God, there is no mistaking the love that is
at the root of every word you speak to me in
Christ. I want my words to have the same origin,
and clearly express the love that you are bringing
to fullness in me. *Amen.*

"Nothing"

Read 1 Corinthians 13:2

If I speak God's Word with power,
    revealing all his mysteries and making
    everything plain as day, and if I have
    faith that says to a mountain, "Jump,"
    and it jumps, but I don't love, I'm
    nothing.

1 Corinthians 13:2

Spiritual arithmetic is no substitute for love: powerful prophecy added to expert knowledge, added to mountain-moving faith, minus love, equals zero. The absence of love is an absence of meaning—a black hole at the center of things.

Do you ever separate spiritual works from loving acts?

PRAYER: Father, instead of letting myself be dazzled by the supernatural, help me to be disciplined to acts of love. Just as everything you say and do in Christ is an act of love, so let me also speak and act out of a similar reality. *Amen.*

"Don't Love"

Read 1 Corinthians 13:3

If I give everything I own to the poor and
even go to the stake to be burned as
a martyr, but don't love, I've gotten
nowhere. So, no matter what I say, what
I believe, and what I do, I'm bankrupt
without love.

1 Corinthians 13:3

The most lavish gifts of money or material posses-
sions cannot substitute for love. A life offered up
in the most extravagant sacrifice cannot substitute
for love. Try as we might, we cannot find a substitute for love.

What do you try to substitute for love?

PRAYER: But I do try to find substitutes, Lord. I try
to substitute things or deeds or symbols. Anything to avoid the risk and venture and pain of
love. Forgive me for my recalcitrance and return
me to the way of love. *Amen.*

"Love . . ."

Read 1 Corinthians 13:4–6

Love never gives up. Love cares more for
others than for self. Love doesn't want
what it doesn't have. Love doesn't strut.

I Corinthians 13:4

Love is not a romantic frill but a workaday necessity. It is not a feeling in the moonlight but God's way of being with another in the rough-and-tumble realities of human relationships.

How many items are in Paul's description?

PRAYER: I am always pushing love out to the edges of life, dear God, reducing it to a feeling; and you keep bringing it back into the center where it is an action. I want to exchange my shallow frivolities for your deep realities; in the name of Jesus. *Amen.*

"Always"

Read 1 Corinthians 13:7

[Love]
Puts up with anything,
Trusts God always,
Always looks for the best,
Never looks back,
But keeps going to the end.

1 Corinthians 13:7

Always? Yes, always. There is nothing that life presents to us that cannot be met and dealt with in love. If we think otherwise, it is not because we know more about life than Paul knew, but because we know less about love.

What do you tend to exclude from love?

PRAYER: Lord Jesus Christ, when I come across things or people that I don't want to or can't seem to love, show me how you do it, and why you do it. *Amen.*

"When the Complete Arrives"
Read 1 Corinthians 13:8–10

But when the Complete arrives, our
incompletes will be canceled.

1 Corinthians 13:10

Each gift is partial and only useful as a means to
the goal. Love is the goal. Gifts are only good insofar as they help us to arrive at or express love.

Are you easily distracted from the goal?

PRAYER: Father in heaven, I get so wrapped up in
my own projects and enthusiasms that I forget the
big picture—forget that the gifts you give and the
tasks you assign are only steps on the way of experiencing and expressing the love you reveal in
your Son. *Amen.*

AUGUST 9

"Left Those Infant Ways"
Read 1 Corinthians 13:11

When I was an infant at my mother's
breast, I gurgled and cooed like any
infant. When I grew up, I left those
infant ways for good.

1 Corinthians 13:11

Christian experience *develops*: aptitudes mature into
responsibilities; an absorption in self changes into
a concern for others; sporadic enthusiasms acquire a sustained intensity. If what is charming in
childhood does not mature, it loses its charm and
becomes only an embarrassment.

Compare this with Hebrews 6:1–3.

PRAYER: Thank you, Lord, for every good gift and
every delightful experience. Now use what you
have given to bring me to new levels of trust and
obedience, even to maturity in Christ. *Amen.*

AUGUST 10

"Just as He Knows Us"
Read 1 Corinthians 13:12

We don't yet see things clearly. We're
squinting in a fog, peering through a
mist. But it won't be long before the
weather clears and the sun shines bright!
We'll see it all then, see it all as clearly as
God sees us, knowing him directly just
as he knows us!

1 Corinthians 13:12

To be known is fundamental to knowing. Only
when we are confident that we are thoroughly
known by God are we free and motivated to em-
bark on a lifetime of deepening knowledge of God.
What does God know about you?

PRAYER: As I understand more, O God, help me to
love more. As I learn to comprehend your ways,
use my new knowledge to deepen faith and to en-
large hope. *Amen.*

"The Best of the Three"
Read 1 Corinthians 13:13

But for right now, until that completeness,
    we have three things to do to lead us
    toward that consummation: Trust steadily
    in God, hope unswervingly, love extrav-
    agantly. And the best of the three is love.
                                    1 Corinthians 13:13

Christ eliminates the clutter from our lives. The wind of the Spirit blows away the mist of the world's vanity and reveals in gospel sunlight the great and shining realities.

What do you no longer need?

PRAYER: God, how simple things become when I see it your way. How many things I no longer have to do; how many things I no longer need! Now I am free to do the one thing needful and, undistracted, enjoy your love. *Amen.*

"Go After a Life of Love"

Read 1 Corinthians 14:1

Go after a life of love as if your life
depended on it—because it does. Give
yourselves to the gifts God gives you.
Most of all, try to proclaim his truth.

1 Corinthians 14:1

Will we let others impose their craven choices on
us, or will *we* choose? Will we permit the world to
persuade us of the importance of trivia, or will *we*
tell the world what is important? To aim for anything other than love is to aim too low.

Is love your aim?

PRAYER: I am immersed, Lord, in mediocrity. But
I won't settle for less than you have promised. You
have shown me what is best, in the name of Jesus
Christ. *Amen.*

"Everyday Speech"
Read 1 Corinthians 14:2–5

> But when you proclaim his truth in every-
> day speech, you're letting others in on the
> truth so that they can grow and be strong
> and experience his presence with you.
>
> 1 Corinthians 14:3

The Christian faith is thoroughly and insistently
practical. Basically, it is not what makes us feel
good or what dazzles others, but what builds a life
of faith and hope and love. Being a Christian is
more like being a carpenter of the virtues than a
dilettante of the emotions.

How many times is the word "proclaim" used
here?

PRAYER: Father, I keep coming to these forks in the
road, having to choose between indulging myself
and building up another, between feeling good
and being good. Help me to make constructive
choices for the sake of Jesus Christ. Amen.

AUGUST 14

"Can't Be Distinguished"
Read 1 Corinthians 14:6–12

If musical instruments—flutes, say, or
  harps—aren't played so that each note
  is distinct and in tune, how will anyone
  be able to catch the melody and enjoy
  the music? If the trumpet call can't be
  distinguished, will anyone show up for
  the battle?

1 Corinthians 14:8

Speech is one of the most marvelous of gifts. Ecstatic speech ("tongues") is not without its value; but our deepest interest must be in using words that will convey as clearly as possible the good news of God's love and salvation.

What is God's clearest word to you?

PRAYER: Because words are easily spoken, Lord, I overlook the overwhelming significance of the clearly spoken and clearly understood word. Your word brought both creation and salvation into existence; use my words to let others know what you speak, and what happens when you speak. Amen.

"Five Words"
Read 1 Corinthians 14:13–19

But when I'm in a church assembled for
worship, I'd rather say five words that
everyone can understand and learn from
than say ten thousand that sound to
others like gibberish.

1 Corinthians 14:19

W. R. Inge, himself a thorough believer in the supernatural, warned against "the old hankerings after supernatural manifestations, which are always dear to semi-regenerate minds." The words the Spirit gives us to use with others are plain speech, for the plain communication of God's truth and love.

Do you speak plainly?

PRAYER: Your word, Almighty God, is clear enough: you speak love and mercy and judgment and forgiveness. I want to share those words. I will speak no more than I know, but, at the same time, no less than I know. *Amen.*

"Use Your Head"
Read 1 Corinthians 14:20–25

To be perfectly frank, I'm getting exasper-
   ated with your infantile thinking. How
   long before you grow up and use your
   head—your *adult* head? It's all right to
   have a childlike unfamiliarity with evil;
   a simple *no* is all that's needed there. But
   there's far more to saying *yes* to something. Only mature and well-exercised
   intelligence can save you from falling
   into gullibility.

1 Corinthians 14:20

The life of the mind does not atrophy as life in the
Spirit develops. Thinking cannot be subtracted
from being. As the Spirit fills us with new life and
power, he also brings new life to the mind so that
we can understand the ways of the "Word becoming flesh and blood" among us.

What scripture does Paul quote?

PRAYER: "Take Thou our minds, dear Lord, we
humbly pray; Give us the mind of Christ each
passing day; Teach us to know the truth that sets us
free; Grant us in all our thoughts to honor Thee"
(William Hiram Foulkes, "Take Thou Our Minds,
Dear Lord," *The Hymnbook*, 306). *Amen.*

"When You Gather for Worship"
Read 1 Corinthians 14:26–32

> So here's what I want you to do. When
> you gather for worship, each one of
> you be prepared with something that
> will be useful for all: Sing a hymn, teach
> a lesson, tell a story, lead a prayer, provide
> an insight.

> 1 Corinthians 14:26

Each act of worship is an opportunity to bring out into the open what God has placed in our hearts: praise, insight, knowledge, commitment. We share God's gifts with each other and discover our place in Christ's body.

What gifts do you bring to worship?

PRAYER: When I next go to worship, Lord, I want to be prepared: my heart tuned for praise, my mouth ready for witness, my ears ready to listen, my whole self an offering for love and faith. Help me to do that in Jesus' name. *Amen.*

"God Doesn't Stir Us Up"
Read 1 Corinthians 14:33–36

God doesn't stir us up into confusion;
  he brings us into harmony. This goes
  for all the churches—no exceptions.
                            1 Corinthians 14:33

Worship is that act by which we submit ourselves to God's order, God's beauty, and God's word. It is not an excuse to flaunt our opinions or assert our egos. We don't come to hang out our dirty laundry but to put on new robes of righteousness.

What do you think may have been happening in the Corinthian church?

PRAYER: Father, create an orderly and submissive mind in me so that when I come to worship with brothers and sisters in Christ I may fit into the design that you are making, glad to realize what you have planned for me before the foundation of the world. *Amen.*

"Courteous and Considerate"
Read 1 Corinthians 14:37–40

Be courteous and considerate in everything.
1 Corinthians 14:40

Spiritual gifts are not trophies to be put on display. Our maturity is in evidence only insofar as we obey. Every time we attract attention to ourselves we are a distraction. Only when our gifts are submitted to Christ's direction do they fulfill their intent.

What is the command that Paul gives?

PRAYER: Dear Lord Jesus, command me and teach me obedience. Direct me and show me submission. I offer up to you all that you have given to me that it might fit into your ordered ways in a pattern of holiness. Amen.

"Let Me Go Over the Message"
Read 1 Corinthians 15:1–2

Friends, let me go over the Message with
you one final time—this Message that
I proclaimed and that you made your
own; this Message on which you took
your stand and by which your life has
been saved. (I'm assuming, now, that
your belief was the real thing and not
a passing fancy, that you're in this for
good and holding fast.)

1 Corinthians 15:1–2

We need repeated reminders: the life of faith begins and continues in relation to what God has
done in Christ. It is not advice, it is not information, it is *news*. "Gospel" is the good news of what
God has done and does and will do, not a com-
mentary on what we do.

What three terms does Paul emphasize?

PRAYER: God, I am always getting more interested
in my ideas than in your truth, paying more attention to my feelings than to your action, caught
up in making plans rather than in searching out
your will. Remind me of what I first heard with
gladness; return me to my center in Christ. *Amen.*

"The First Thing"
Read 1 Corinthians 15:3–11

> The first thing I did was place before you
> what was placed so emphatically before
> me: that the Messiah died for our sins,
> exactly as Scripture tells us; that he was
> buried; that he was raised from death on
> the third day, again exactly as Scripture
> says; that he presented himself alive to
> Peter, then to his closest followers.
>
> 1 Corinthians 15:3–5

Death and life, the boundaries of existence, are the essential realities with which we all have to deal. Under the forms of crucifixion and resurrection, Christ experienced them deeply and absolutely, and in such a way as to make a gospel out of them.

How many resurrection appearances does Paul list?

PRAYER: Christ, I try but cannot avoid death. I strive for and cannot achieve life. And then I hear that you have changed it all for me—conquered death and seized life. And then you share it all with me! Thank you. All praise! *Amen.*

"If Christ Wasn't Raised"
Read 1 Corinthians 15:12–19

And if Christ wasn't raised, then all you're
  doing is wandering about in the dark,
  as lost as ever.

1 Corinthians 15:17

Resurrection is the event without which the Christian has nothing distinctive, nothing convincing, nothing hopeful, nothing important to say. It is God's life taking root and blossoming in the desert of human death. It is an explosion of vitality in the emptiness of human futility.

How many times does the word "if" occur? Why is the repetition significant?

PRAYER: Lord, I don't want a minimum religion but a maximum faith. I don't want to just get by on the least common denominator but to live gloriously with the highest degree of intensity. I want to experience resurrection, now and later. *Amen.*

"The First in a Long Legacy"
Read 1 Corinthians 15:20–28

But the truth is that Christ has been raised
up, the first in a long legacy of those
who are going to leave the cemeteries.

1 Corinthians 15:20

We understand our common plight from an examination of Adam; we realize our certain hope in an adoration of Christ. What took place in Christ (namely, resurrection) is not an exception to the rule but the first occurrence of what is repeated in all who participate in his salvation.

What psalm does Paul quote?

PRAYER: Lord, why am I always reducing the great word *"resurrection,"* leaving out large chunks of meaning, missing obvious implications? The evidence in Christ is clear—and grand. After you have made such a beginning, how can I doubt that you will carry it to a magnificent conclusion? *Amen.*

"I Fought the Wild Beasts at Ephesus"
Read 1 Corinthians 15:29–34

> Do you think I was just trying to act heroic
>   when I fought the wild beasts at Ephesus,
>   hoping it wouldn't be the end of me?
> Not on your life! It's resurrection, resur-
>   rection, always resurrection, that under-
>   girds what I do and say, the way I live.
> If there's no resurrection, "We eat, we
>   drink, the next day we die," and that's
>   all there is to it.

1 Corinthians 15:32

If eating and drinking is all there is to life, it makes no sense to risk a good meal or a warm bed for love or truth—or God. The best thing to do is live carefully and comfortably. But no Christian, participant in resurrection, can live so tamely.

How does Paul's life illustrate his counsel?

PRAYER: I want to live this way too, Lord: not calculating the risks or cautiously protecting my interests but adventurously in pursuit of your will, undeterred by opposition, impatient of sin and ardent in faith. *Amen.*

"Some Skeptic Is Sure to Ask"
Read 1 Corinthians 15:35–41

Some skeptic is sure to ask, "Show me how resurrection works. Give me a diagram; draw me a picture. What does this 'resurrection body' look like?"

1 Corinthians 15:35

We can understand the resurrection in terms of earthly experience no more than we can imagine what an apple, say, will look and taste like by looking at an apple seed. This life is the "bare kernel" of what, in the resurrection, will be a glorious wholeness.

What illustrations does Paul use?

PRAYER: "O what their joy and their glory must be, Those endless Sabbaths the blessed ones see; Crown for the valiant, to weary ones rest; God shall be All, and in all ever blest" (Pierre Abelard, "O What Their Joy and Their Glory Must Be," *The Hymnbook*, 424). *Amen.*

"Embrace Our Heavenly Ends"
Read 1 Corinthians 15:42–50

In the same way that we've worked from
our earthy origins, let's embrace our
heavenly ends.

1 Corinthians 15:49

The resurrection Jesus is "made out of heaven."
He is now our ancestor rather than Adam. It is no
longer Adam's sin, which consigns us to dust, that
is definitive but the new Adam's resurrection,
which puts us in heavenly places.

How many contrasts can you find in this passage?

PRAYER: Lord Jesus Christ, I offer this body to you
as seed for eternity. Arrange the materials of this
life into the image of the Man "made out of
heaven" as I, in faith and by grace, anticipate what
it means to live in glory and honor, inheriting the
imperishable. *Amen.*

"All Going to Be Changed"
Read 1 Corinthians 15:51–57

But let me tell you something wonderful,
a mystery I'll probably never fully understand. We're not all going to die—but we
are all going to be changed.

1 Corinthians 15:51

Resurrection is change from the worse to the better, from the inevitabilities of death to the im-
mensities of life. Existence is not an agonizing
deterioration into despair, a "terminal illness"
(Samuel Beckett), but a developing faith and hope
in the God who completes his victory personally
in us.

Read Isaiah 25:8, the passage Paul quotes.

PRAYER: Thank you, God, for the victory. I do not
understand it, but I am confident in it. I do not
know how it happens, only that it happens. Already in Jesus Christ you have made resurrection
the great and controlling reality of my life, throwing death and sin into the shadows. Amen.

"Throw Yourselves into the Work"
Read 1 Corinthians 15:58

With all this going for us, my dear, dear
friends, stand your ground. And don't
hold back. Throw yourselves into the
work of the Master, confident that
nothing you do for him is a waste of
time or effort.

1 Corinthians 15:58

The resurrection changes the present from a time
of emptiness and futility to a time of abounding
fullness and purpose. The remembered resurrection of Christ and the anticipated resurrection of
the Christian are converging lines that meet and
fill the present with hearty energy.

How does resurrection change your present life?

PRAYER: Lead me into the full meaning of resurrection today, Lord. I want to experience how
what happened to you one day in Palestine, and
what will be completed in me one day in heaven,
can give vitality and steadiness to life now. Amen.

"Regarding the Relief Offering"
Read 1 Corinthians 16:1–4

Regarding the relief offering for poor
Christians that is being collected, you
get the same instructions I gave the
churches in Galatia.

1 Corinthians 16:1

When the Christians at Jerusalem were hard-pressed financially because of persecution and prejudice, brothers and sisters in Christ from Galatia to Greece made contributions to assist them. To this day, the offering is a typical act of Christian worship. Christians care and Christians give.

Why do you give your money away?

PRAYER: "All things are Thine; no gift have we, Lord of all gifts, to offer Thee; And hence with grateful hearts today Thine own before Thy feet we lay" (John Greenleaf Whittier, "All Things Are Thine," *The Hymnbook*, 555). *Amen.*

"A Huge Door"
Read 1 Corinthians 16:5–9

For the present, I'm staying right here in
Ephesus. A huge door of opportunity for
good work has opened up here. (There
is also mushrooming opposition.)
1 Corinthians 16:8–9

Paul's leadership combined two essential aspects
of Christian ministry: an intense caring that de-
veloped deep relationships within the churches,
and an adventurous reaching out that crossed
frontiers and shared the good news with others.
He was equally concerned with the church's health
and the world's salvation.

Compare this with Revelation 3:7–8.

PRAYER: Lord, keep me alert in both directions: in
touch with my faith friends, caring for and loving
them; and in search of people whom you are
preparing to hear the good news, witnessing and
helping them. *Amen.*

"If Timothy Shows Up"
Read 1 Corinthians 16:10–14

If Timothy shows up, take good care of
him. Make him feel completely at home
among you. He works so hard for the
Master, just as I do.

1 Corinthians 16:10

Were the Corinthians disappointed that the elo-
quent Apollos was not going to visit them? Did
they see Timothy as an uninteresting substitute?
But the church is a family, not a theater. Leaders
are not performers but brothers and sisters. Simple hospitality, not an elaborate protocol, must
guide our relations.

What do you know about Apollos? About Timothy?

PRAYER: Lord, I want to practice the skills of hospitality today, putting each guest in my home at
ease, making each visitor in my church welcome;
not lifting one person up and putting down another, but greeting all in Christ's name. *Amen.*

"Hello"
Read 1 Corinthians 16:15–20

The churches here in western Asia send
greetings. Aquila, Priscilla, and the
church that meets in their house say
hello.

1 Corinthians 16:19

Behind the exchange of greetings we sense a vibrant community of people who care for, pray for, and serve one another. The church, then and now, is a place where we expect and bring out the best in one another.

What are some names important to you in your faith?

PRAYER: God, I thank you for friends who recognize me, who know my name, and who greet me with heartiness. In my own way help me to do it too, letting each person I meet know that he is important, that she is significant. *Amen.*

"Make Room for the Master"
Read 1 Corinthians 16:21–24

If anyone won't love the Master, throw
him out. Make room for the Master!
1 Corinthians 16:22

In the midst of all the comings and goings of the
traveling Christians mentioned in this conclusion,
one coming overshadows all the rest and charges
them with hope—the coming again of Christ.
The prayer is still the Christian's hope.

What are two ways the word "love" is used
here?

PRAYER: Make room for the Master! Our Lord,
come! Finish your work. Fulfill the promises. Reap
the harvest. Complete creation. Our Lord, come!
Amen.

"God's Congregation in Corinth"
Read 2 Corinthians 1:1–2

I, Paul, have been sent on a special mission
by the Messiah, Jesus, planned by God
himself. I write this to God's congregation in Corinth, and to believers all over
Achaia province.

2 Corinthians 1:1

God's will, God's church, God's grace, God's peace:
these are Paul's subjects as he writes this letter of
wise and skillful direction for people who want to
live by faith, in love.

What do you know about the church in Corinth?

PRAYER: Speak to me, Holy Spirit, with these very
words that you inspired Paul to write so long ago.
Use them to deepen my relationship with my Lord
and nourish my growth in the faith, in my Savior's
name. *Amen.*

"God of All Healing Counsel"
Read 2 Corinthians 1:3–4

All praise to the God and Father of our
Master, Jesus the Messiah! Father of all
mercy! God of all healing counsel!
2 Corinthians 1:3

Comfort is the prominent theme here: God is not
remote, but near; God is not indifferent, but caring; God is not abstract, but personal. The gospel
is first the declaration and then the experience of
a God who makes a difference in our lives, a God
who makes us better, makes us able.

How many times is the idea of "comfort" used
here?

PRAYER: God of all comfort, you not only stand
alongside me, supporting me with your goodness
and strength, you equip me to do the same thing
for another. Use every experience of comfort I
have to bring comfort to someone who needs it.
Amen.

SEPTEMBER 5

"It Works Out"

Read 2 Corinthians 1:5

When we suffer for Jesus, it works out for
your healing and salvation. If we are
treated well, given a helping hand and
encouraging word, that also works to
your benefit, spurring you on, face
forward, unflinching.

2 Corinthians 1:5

Everything increases and intensifies in the life of
faith in Christ: suffering and comfort; the pains of
the world's hurts and the consolations of the Savior's salvation; a sense of the awful waste of sin
and the experience of abundant blessing.

How does Christ change your life?

PRAYER: Let grace abound in me, O Christ: I would
feel everything there is to feel, see everything there
is to see, taste it all, grasp it all. I don't want to
sleepwalk through this glorious world you have
created and redeemed; I want to be awake and
praise. *Amen.*

"You're Going to Make It"
Read 2 Corinthians 1:6–7

When we see that you're just as willing to
endure the hard times as to enjoy the
good times, we know you're going to
make it, no doubt about it.

2 Corinthians 1:7

The task of the Christian is not to avoid suffering,
but to suffer for the right things—to share the
sufferings of Christ and the community of Christ.
We do not doubt God's love or Christ's presence at
every new sign of trouble; hope is not built on the
pleasure principle, but on Christ's life.

What were some of Paul's sufferings?

PRAYER: Whose sufferings can I share, Lord? Lead
me to someone today who needs help in carrying
a burden, or who needs a companion through
the valley of shadows, or who needs to experience
hope in a fresh way. *Amen.*

"It *Was* So Bad"
Read 2 Corinthians 1:8–10

We don't want you in the dark, friends,
  about how hard it was when all this
  came down on us in Asia province.
It was so bad we didn't think we were
  going to make it.

2 Corinthians 1:8

Extremities of trouble taught Paul that God does what humanity cannot do: he raises the dead; he saves us from despair. When we no longer can help ourselves, he helps us.

What has been your worst trouble?

PRAYER: Father in heaven, use the disappointments, the troubles, the difficulties that I run into, and that my friends run into, to lead us into new experiences of resurrection, in which you act to bring life and establish hope. *Amen.*

"You and Your Prayers"
Read 2 Corinthians 1:11

You and your prayers are part of the rescue
operation—I don't want you in the dark
about that either. I can see your faces
even now, lifted in praise for God's deliverance of us, a rescue in which your
prayers played such a crucial part.
2 Corinthians 1:11

Prayer is not an afterthought in the Christian life. It
is not pious embroidery to good deeds. It is working at the center: acts are performed and words
spoken, but prayer is our participation in the divine causality, firsthand.

Who are you praying for today?

PRAYER: Lord, I get so impatient merely praying: I
want to do something big, say something significant. Return me to my knees to the action and
speech of prayer, where "more things are wrought
than this world dreams of" (Tennyson). Amen.

SEPTEMBER 9

"It Was God"
Read 2 Corinthians 1:12

Now that the worst is over, we're pleased
we can report that we've come out of
this with conscience and faith intact,
and can face the world—and even more
importantly, face you with our heads
held high. But it wasn't by any fancy
footwork on our part. It was God who
kept us focused on him, uncompromised.
2 Corinthians 1:12

Christian behavior is not calculating or shrewd—
it is not designed to get things or to make things
happen. It is, rather, personal and reverent, affirming the goodness in people and things and accepting God's presence there.

Compare this with 1 Corinthians 2:1–5.

PRAYER: All-wise God, make me wise so that my
life may be a channel for your wisdom wherever I
am today, for whomever I am with. Give me a sense
of the high holiness in all creation and every creature so that I live always in awe and praise. Amen.

"See the Whole Picture"
Read 2 Corinthians 1:13–14

Don't try to read between the lines or
 look for hidden meanings in this letter.
 We're writing plain, unembellished
 truth, hoping that you'll now see the
 whole picture as well as you've seen
 some of the details.

2 Corinthians 1:13

There are some who speak in complicated and dark mysteries, and call it religion. The gospel is marked by clarity and simplicity. If there are mysteries here, they are mysteries of light, not darkness.

What don't you understand?

PRAYER: Thank you, Lord Jesus Christ, for plain words and acts that I can read and follow. Thank you for coming to my level and addressing me in common speech. Help me to express my thanks plainly and in common things. *Amen.*

SEPTEMBER 11

"Being Flip with My Promises"
Read 2 Corinthians 1:15–18

Are you now going to accuse me of being
flip with my promises because it didn't
work out? Do you think I talk out of
both sides of my mouth—a glib *yes* one
moment, a glib *no* the next?

2 Corinthians 1:17

For Paul, traveling was not tourism but apostleship.
What looked like indecisiveness—some had appar-
ently accused him of being wishy-washy—was, in
fact, readiness to be both directed and redirected by
God. Our plans, no matter how much we have in-
vested in them, need to be submitted to our faithful Lord.

Do you permit God to change your plans?

PRAYER: I submit this day's plans to you, Lord. You
know what I want to do and what I need to do.
Help me to be undeviating in my purpose but also
flexible in responding to the unexpected that you
introduce into my routine. *Amen.*

"A Clean, Strong Yes"
Read 2 Corinthians 1:19–22

When Silas and Timothy and I proclaimed
the Son of God among you, did you pick
up on any yes-and-no, on-again, off-
again waffling? Wasn't it a clean, strong
Yes?

2 Corinthians 1:19

Amen is the Hebrew word for yes. At the center of
the Christian gospel there is this great, repeated,
resounding, all-encompassing affirmation. God
says yes to us; we say yes to him. Yes! Amen!

How does God say yes to you?

PRAYER: Thank you for your yes, faithful God: including me, accepting me, affirming me. Turn all
my cautious, wary, hesitating responses into a
likewise hearty yes, my whole life an answering
Amen! Amen.

"By Your Own Faith"
Read 2 Corinthians 1:23–24

We're partners, working alongside you,
joyfully expectant. I know that you stand
by your own faith, not by ours.

2 Corinthians 1:24

All Christians are colleagues: none is superior to another; none is inferior to another. Each of us has a gift of ministry with which we serve another; none of us is provided a position from which to lord it over another.

What is one of your ways of working with others for their joy?

PRAYER: O God, sometimes people build me up so I think I am better than they are. Others tear me down and I think I am worse than they are. You, Lord, make me companion to them with commands and opportunities to work with them for their joy—which gives *me* joy. *Amen.*

SEPTEMBER 14

"My Reason for Writing"
Read 2 Corinthians 2:1–4

That was my reason for writing a letter
instead of coming—so I wouldn't have
to spend a miserable time disappointing
the very friends I had looked forward to
cheering me up. I was convinced at the
time I wrote it that what was best for me
was also best for you.

2 Corinthians 2:3

An earlier letter to the Corinthians was a sharply
worded reprimand, causing pain. There can be no
deepening of the common life of the Spirit unless
there is a facing and dealing with sin; no growth
without pain. But such pain is always shared pain.
The Corinthians must know that even though Paul
administered it, he also shared it.

From whom have you received a painful but
necessary rebuke?

PRAYER: I am grateful, God, to your servants who
have had the courage and sensitivity to face me
with my faults and sins and immaturities. Even
though it was painful to them and to me, great joy
has come of it. Thank you. *Amen*

SEPTEMBER 15

"Enough"
Read 2 Corinthians 2:5–8

What the majority of you agreed to as
punishment is punishment enough.
2 Corinthians 2:6

Reprimands must be administered, but they must
also be terminated. Rebukes must not become rejections. We require punishment, but forgiveness
and love always have the last word in the community of Christ.

To whom must you say no?

PRAYER: I thank you, Lord, that your no is always
followed by a yes, that your disapproval of my actions is never a rejection of me. "Faithful are the
wounds of a friend!" (Proverbs 27:6). *Amen.*

"Not Oblivious to His Sly Ways"
Read 2 Corinthians 2:9–11

> The fact is that I'm joining in with your forgiveness, as Christ is with us, guiding us. After all, we don't want to unwittingly give Satan an opening for yet more mischief—we're not oblivious to his sly ways!
>
> 2 Corinthians 2:10–11

Not vindictive punishment, nor righteous indignation, but forgiveness is the grand strategy of the gospel. Any other method for dealing with sin and sinners ends up by making things worse than ever.

What are some of Satan's sly ways?

PRAYER: Father in heaven, train me in your methods of expressing love by forgiveness, so that the people around me are drawn deeper into the ways of grace, not further tangled in the web of Satan. In the name of Jesus Christ. *Amen.*

SEPTEMBER 17

"Didn't Find Titus"
Read 2 Corinthians 2:12–13

> But when I didn't find Titus waiting for me
> with news of your condition, I couldn't
> relax. Worried about you, I left and
> came on to Macedonia province looking
> for Titus and a reassuring word on you.
>   2 Corinthians 2:13

Pioneer as Paul was, he was not alone: he sought out companions in ministry who became brothers. All the evidence shows that Paul shared both responsibility and authority readily and easily.

Where is Troas? What is Macedonia?

PRAYER: As I seek to be obedient to your call in me, O Christ, and as you provide me with brothers and sisters who share love and mercy, create among us a community that does honor to your name. *Amen.*

"A Sweet Scent"
Read 2 Corinthians 2:14–16

Because of Christ, we give off a sweet scent
rising to God, which is recognized by
those on the way of salvation—an aroma
redolent with life. But those on the way
to destruction treat us more like the
stench from a rotting corpse. This is a
terrific responsibility. Is anyone competent to take it on?

2 Corinthians 2:15–16

The same atmosphere that is pleasant to some is
offensive to others; a fragrance that evokes antici-
pation in one precipitates dread in another. Such
is the atmosphere of life accompanying those who
love and speak the life of Christ.

Why are some people offended by Christ?

PRAYER: "Master, no offering costly and sweet, May
we, like Magdalene, Lay at Thy feet; Yet may love's
incense rise, Sweeter than sacrifice, dear Lord, to
Thee, Dear Lord, to Thee" (Edwin P. Parker, "Master, No Offering Costly and Sweet," The Hymnbook,
299). Amen.

SEPTEMBER 19

"Sell It Cheap"

Read 2 Corinthians 2:17

No—but at least we don't take God's
Word, water it down, and then take it to
the streets to sell it cheap. We stand in
Christ's presence when we speak; God
looks us in the face. We get what we say
straight from God and say it as honestly
as we can.

2 Corinthians 2:17

The blight of commercialism on the church today
is not new: Paul was distressed by it in the first
century. We, like Paul, must put as much distance
as possible between ourselves and those who use
positions of religious leadership to line their own
pockets.

What "peddler of God's word" has distressed
you?

PRAYER: God, you give and I receive: it is all grace
on your part, all faith on mine. What I have received freely, let me give freely. I want to be spontaneous in my generosity, not calculating in my
acquisitiveness; I want my life to be characterized
by giving, not getting. For Jesus' sake. Amen.

"Carved into Human Lives"
Read 2 Corinthians 3:1–3

Your very lives are a letter that anyone
can read by just looking at you. Christ
himself wrote it—not with ink, but
with God's living Spirit; not chiseled
into stone, but carved into human
lives—and we publish it.

2 Corinthians 3:3

Paul has no need of formal letters of commendation or approval. People who have been instructed by his teaching and led by his direction are "letters" that can be read by any who wish. These are the certificates that legitimize his ministry.

What sort of "letter" are you?

PRAYER: Father in heaven, when others find fault with me, I don't want to be reduced by that criticism into self-justifying or rationalizing behavior. I want to be free to live spontaneously under your mercy, confident that your Holy Spirit will make plain in people of faith the truth of your word. *Amen.*

"Only God"

Read 2 Corinthians 3:4–6

We couldn't be more sure of ourselves in
this—that *you*, written by Christ himself
for God, are our letter of recommen-
dation. We wouldn't think of writing
this kind of letter about ourselves. Only
God can write such a letter.

2 Corinthians 3:4–5

Paul's assurance is not self-confidence but God-
confidence. He has discovered something better
than his own abilities, namely, the gifts of the
Holy Spirit. Not by what people say about him,
not by what he feels within himself, but in what
God gives, he does his work.

What are your qualifications?

PRAYER: Dear God, I know that your gifts must
never be used as an excuse for not developing my
own abilities; but I also know that my abilities
must never become a substitute for centering my
life in your Spirit, the fountain of life. *Amen.*

SEPTEMBER 22

"How Much More"
Read 2 Corinthians 3:7–11

> If that makeshift arrangement impressed
> us, how much more this brightly
> shining government installed for
> eternity?

2 Corinthians 3:11

The life of faith is access to splendor. It is never a constriction but always an expansion. Sin reduces life to black-and-white; grace recovers the entire spectrum of color that is in creation and salvation.

Do you live in black-and-white or in full color?

PRAYER: Lord Jesus Christ, through sin-dulled eyes I look out on a drab, flat world: heal my vision so that I see all the colors and all the dimensions in the world where you love and save and bless. *Amen.*

"Only Christ Can Get Rid of the Veil"
Read 2 Corinthians 3:12–17

Only Christ can get rid of the veil so they
can see for themselves that there's
nothing there.

2 Corinthians 3:16

The old covenant revealed to Moses is compared
with the new covenant in Christ: the comparison
is not between true and false but between the
clear and the blurred, the focused and the unfo-
cused. Christ repudiates nothing of Moses; he
clarifies everything.

What has Christ clarified for you?

PRAYER: Lord Jesus Christ, release me from attach-
ment to old and comfortable truths so that I may
grow, by faith, into the new, challenging, life-
enhancing realities of your Spirit. *Amen.*

"We Are Transfigured"
Read 2 Corinthians 3:18

All of us! Nothing between us and God,
    our faces shining with the brightness of
    his face. And so we are transfigured
    much like the Messiah, our lives gradu-
    ally becoming brighter and more beau-
    tiful as God enters our lives and we
    become like him.

2 Corinthians 3:18

We do not stay the same. As long as we are alive,
we change. But in what way? Do we grow and develop? Or do we deteriorate and diminish? In the
presence of Jesus Christ we grow: we become that
which we behold.

Have you changed in the last year?

PRAYER: By faith, dear Christ, I look and listen and
love: change me into your likeness hour by hour,
day by day. I want to express your will, your truth,
demonstrate your love, you living in me. *Amen.*

"We're Not About To"

Read 2 Corinthians 4:1

Since God has so generously let us in on
what he is doing, we're not about to
throw up our hands and walk off the job
just because we run into occasional hard
times.

2 Corinthians 4:1

All work, for people of faith, is ministry. If the
work is offered to God, we cannot, finally, despair
in it. We can become tired; we can even, perhaps,
become bored. But we cannot despair. He who
commands this work ("the job") provides for its
completion ("God has so generously. . . ").

How is your job of ministry?

PRAYER: Let me, O Christ, see everything I do
today as work done in your service. I offer all my
movements and thoughts and words to you. Make
them a means for creating your kingdom, under
your generosity. *Amen.*

"Maneuver and Manipulate"
Read 2 Corinthians 4:2

We refuse to wear masks and play games.
We don't maneuver and manipulate
behind the scenes. And we don't twist
God's Word to suit ourselves. Rather, we
keep everything we do and say out in the
open, the whole truth on display, so that
those who want to can see and judge for
themselves in the presence of God.

2 Corinthians 4:2

The history of religion is full of instances of people who do the right things using wrong means: who use misleading advertising to raise money for charity, who tell untrue stories to illustrate gospel truths, who hypocritically misrepresent themselves while zealously presenting God's truth. Paul insists that the means is as important as the end.

What right thing have you done the wrong way?

PRAYER: Lord, I want my life to be consistently open, relaxed in the assurance that your truth needs no clever or cunning assistance from me to make its way in the world, but only faithful obedience and faith. *Amen.*

"Stone-Blind"

Read 2 Corinthians 4:3–4

All they have eyes for is the fashionable god
of darkness. They think he can give them
what they want, and that they won't
have to bother believing a Truth they
can't see. They're stone-blind to the
dayspring brightness of the Message that
shines with Christ, who gives us the best
picture of God we'll ever get.

2 Corinthians 4:4

If the gospel is so clear, why do so many not see
it? Unbelief is as incomprehensible to faith as
faith is to unbelief. The difficulty, though, is not
in the clarity of the gospel itself, but in the inter-
ference of "the god of this world."

What does Paul mean by "the fashionable god
of darkness"?

PRAYER: You have given me a clear and shining
revelation of your love and salvation in Jesus
Christ, O God: now give me steady and unblurred
vision so that I may live in the light. *Amen.*

"Not About Ourselves"
Read 2 Corinthians 4:5–6

Remember, our Message is not about
ourselves; we're proclaiming Jesus
Christ, the Master. All we are is mes-
sengers, errand runners from Jesus
for you.

2 Corinthians 4:5

Paul does not have a religious scheme that he is
trying to sell that will improve people's lives; he is
announcing that the glory of God has burst into
the everyday lives of all of us, and that we can live
in light and not in darkness. He is proclaiming an
immense divine fact, not a mere human idea.

How is Jesus light for you?

PRAYER: "Light of light, enlighten me, Now anew
the day is dawning; Sun of grace, the shadows
flee; Brighten Thou my Sabbath morning; With
Thy joyous sunshine blest, Happy is my day of
rest" (Benjamin Schmolck, "Light of Light, Enlighten Me," The Hymnbook, 73). Amen.

SEPTEMBER 29

"Unadorned Clay Pots"
Read 2 Corinthians 4:7

> If you only look at us, you might well miss
> the brightness. We carry this precious
> Message around in the unadorned clay
> pots of our ordinary lives. That's to
> prevent anyone from confusing God's
> incomparable power with us.
>
> 2 Corinthians 4:7

The imperfections and frailties of human beings, like Paul, who preach and teach are not short-comings to be deplored; they are protection from yet another distraction to worshiping and serving God himself. There was a saying in the early church that the best bishop was a bad bishop—that way, there was no danger of substituting him for the living God.

What were some of Paul's shortcomings?

PRAYER: Instead of complaining and criticizing when I find that my fellow Christians have faults, O God, I will give you thanks for them, knowing that I have found one more stimulus to look to you, O God, and not to human beings, for my help and my salvation. *Amen.*

"But"

Read 2 Corinthians 4:8–12

We've been surrounded and battered by
   troubles, but we're not demoralized;
   we're not sure what to do, but we know
   that God knows what to do; we've been
   spiritually terrorized, but God hasn't left
   our side; we've been thrown down, but
   we haven't broken.

2 Corinthians 4:8–9

The gospel is caught in a conjunction: but. Circumstances affect us; they do not determine us.
Troubles give us pain; they cannot separate us
from the love and purposes of God. "But" separates what the world does to us from what God
does in us, and contrasts them gloriously.

How many contrasts are listed here?

PRAYER: "When the woes of life o'er-take me,
Hopes deceive, and fears annoy, Never shall the
cross forsake me: Lo! it glows with peace and joy.
Bane and blessing, pain and pleasure, By the cross
are sanctified; Peace is there that knows no mea-
sure, Joys that through all time abide" (John
Bowring, "In the Cross of Christ I Glory," *The
Hymnbook*, 195). *Amen.*

"Every Detail Works"
Read 2 Corinthians 4:13–15

Every detail works to your advantage and to
God's glory: more and more grace, more
and more people, more and more praise!
2 Corinthians 4:15

One of Paul's strategies is to provide a sense of
continuity so that we see our origins centuries
ago in the lives of people of faith, and anticipate a
long continuation into the future with "every detail working." We need to be rescued from the ups
and downs of an emotional religion, determined
by whim and weather, measured by impulse and
mood, and be lifted into the wisdom of the centuries.

What scripture does Paul quote?

PRAYER: Integrate me, O God, into your consistent
and faithful ways so that I am not thrown off my
stride by a headline, or a mood, or a criticism, or
a disappointment. Interpret my life to me in the
context of the everlasting hills and the eternal
promises. *Amen.*

"We're Not Giving Up"

Read 2 Corinthians 4:16

> So we're not giving up. How could we!
>   Even though on the outside it often
>   looks like things are falling apart on us,
>   on the inside, where God is making
>   new life, not a day goes by without his
>   unfolding grace.
>
> 2 Corinthians 4:16

A companion with courage is the best companion. A person who faces the worst along with us, and does it with hope and joy, is a priceless friend. Paul's confident courage continues to encourage.

Who is the most encouraging person you know?

PRAYER: God, I want to develop and share such a courage: a heart-confidence that your will always is completed and that your resurrection life always breaks forth, despite feelings and despite appearances. *Amen.*

OCTOBER 3

"The Coming Good Times"
Read 2 Corinthians 4:17–18

These hard times are small potatoes
    compared to the coming good times,
    the lavish celebration prepared for us.
                    2 Corinthians 4:17

We live in a larger world than we can see. We grow in a reality far exceeding what we can measure or describe. We are participants in the glory—the majestic, weighty, eternal ways of the God who loves and saves us in Jesus Christ.

What do the words "coming good times" mean to you?

PRAYER: Accepting your invitation, Lord of life, I will live abundantly, not poorly; gloriously, not meagerly; deeply, not flippantly. I plunge into the ocean of your glory and find myself lifted and laved in the waters of love. Thank you. *Amen.*

"An Unfurnished Shack"
Read 2 Corinthians 5:1–5

> Compared to what's coming, living
> conditions around here seem like a
> stopover in an unfurnished shack, and
> we're tired of it! We've been given a
> glimpse of the real thing, our true
> home, our resurrection bodies!
>
> 2 Corinthians 5:4

The "mortal" is not discarded in the life to come;
it is fulfilled. Meanwhile, there is tension between
the limitations of our creation and the boundless-
ness of eternity, between our fallen condition and
a redeemed people.

Why do you believe in the life to come?

PRAYER: In my hope of more, O God, I will not be
overly impatient with this body of mine, nor of
this history in which I live. But neither will I be
smugly content with it. You have instilled in me a
longing for more: I will now live the longing in
grateful hope under the guarantees of your Spirit.
Amen.

"Exile for Homecoming"
Read 2 Corinthians 5:6–9

When the time comes, we'll be plenty
ready to exchange exile for home-
coming.

2 Corinthians 5:9

If we complain of our mortality, we complain
against the God who ordered it. Of course we
want to be complete in the eternal presence of the
Lord of glory. But there is a life to be lived in faith.
We are "on assignment"—our longing to be at
home with the Lord must not be allowed to interfere with our discipleship here and now.

What are the two ways Paul expresses his con-
tentment?

PRAYER: You have created an eternal home for me,
O God; you have also created a mortal body for
me. I want to be equally at home here and there,
pleasing you in present faith and in unflagging
hope. *Amen.*

"Face God"

Read 2 Corinthians 5:10

Sooner or later we'll all have to face God,
    regardless of our conditions. We will
    appear before Christ and take what's
    coming to us as a result of our actions,
    either good or bad.

2 Corinthians 5:10

For the Christian, living under the mercy of the cross, judgment is a welcome prospect: a final scene in which all the seemingly random threads of our bodily life are suddenly perceived as a tapestry of grace.

Why is judgment to be welcomed, not feared?

PRAYER: I live, Almighty God, in confidence that your decisions will be seen, finally, by everyone to be best and righteous and blessed. Meanwhile, as seeing through a glass darkly, I will live and love and believe in hope. *Amen.*

OCTOBER 7

"One Man Died for Everyone"
Read 2 Corinthians 5:11–15

Our firm decision is to work from this
focused center: One man died for
everyone. That puts everyone in the
same boat. He included everyone in his
death so that everyone could also be
included in his life, a resurrection life,
a far better life than people ever lived
on their own.

2 Corinthians 5:14

Accusations have been made against Paul, challenging his integrity and sanity. He has been called
crazy, self-serving, proud. But, says Paul, that is not
the point: the point is not in any person's position.
The gospel is not advanced according to human
credentials but by the action of Christ.

What is Paul's central point?

PRAYER: Father in heaven, bring me to an end of
thinking about and trusting in myself and to a beginning of thinking about and trusting in you: a
death to dead-end self-centeredness; a birth into
Christ-centered love. Amen.

"Is Created New"
Read 2 Corinthians 5:16–17

Now we look inside, and what we see is
that anyone united with the Messiah gets
a fresh start, is created new. The old life
is gone; a new life burgeons! Look at it!
                                    2 Corinthians 5:17

In Christ we are given a completely new vantage
point, so that instead of seeing everything from
the perspective of the human, we see all in terms
of God's initiative and plan. What we see clearly
and convincingly is that God is at his work of creation again—in us.

What is God creating in you?

PRAYER: I sing the new creation come in Christ,
praising you, Almighty God, for making me into
what I cannot be by my own moral strength. Continue your creative work, each day making something new to your glory. *Amen.*

OCTOBER 9

"Settled the Relationship"
Read 2 Corinthians 5:18–19

All this comes from the God who settled
the relationship between us and him,
and then called us to settle our relationships with each other.

2 Corinthians 5:19

Life is something in which we participate, but do
not invent. It is what we receive, not what we
manufacture. Too often we think that we have to
figure out ways of dealing with God; the gospel
declares that God deals with us. We do not discover techniques for influencing God; we respond
to God's will and work in us.

What do you understand by "settling the relationship"?

PRAYER: What beauty! what mercy! what goodness! You give, God, and I receive. You make my
life free, put praise on my lips and love in my
heart, so that all is hale and holy. All praise to Father, Son, and Holy Ghost! *Amen.*

OCTOBER 10

"Christ's Representatives"
Read 2 Corinthians 5:20

We're Christ's representatives. God uses us
to persuade men and women to drop
their differences and enter into God's
work of making things right between
them. We're speaking for Christ himself
now: Become friends with God; he's
already a friend with you.

2 Corinthians 5:20

However inadequate we seem, however limited
we are, however unqualified we feel—still God
makes it plain that we are used by him to reach
others with Christ's saving love. With such a com-
mission, no Christian dare grumble about not
having interesting or important work to do!

To whom have you been sent as Christ's ambassador?

PRAYER: Lord Christ, I hardly dare to believe that I
am, in fact, your ambassador. Do you really trust
me to speak and act on your behalf? Do you really
think I am capable of sharing your love? Equip me
for the work to which you call me, by your Spirit.
Amen.

"God Put on Him the Wrong"
Read 2 Corinthians 5:21

How? you say. In Christ. God put on him
the wrong who never did anything
wrong, so we could be put right with
God.

2 Corinthians 5:21

A single masterful sentence holds the deep mysteries of the atonement before us. In Christ it is
gathered and absorbed and changed in such a way
that we live now in a radical rightness. The action
is far beyond our understanding but not at all beyond our believing.

When did this happen?

PRAYER: I bring only my sin, Savior Christ, and
leave with only God's righteousness. Not a bad
exchange. I will never understand how it happens, but I will praise you every day that it does
happen. *Amen.*

"Now Is the Right Time"
Read 2 Corinthians 6:1–2

Well, now is the right time to listen,
the day to be helped.

2 Corinthians 6:2

We do not have to spend years qualifying for participation in the gospel. We do not have to go through an elaborate preparation or initiation. We can begin immediately. Now is the point at which eternity invades time.

What scripture does Paul quote?

PRAYER: Sometimes I put off my responses because I don't think I am ready for you, God; other times, because I don't think you are ready for me. Either way, I am wrong: I find that I have wasted good hours, good days, good years when I could be living deeply in love. I will waste no more time, but seize your promised and present life in Christ. Amen.

OCTOBER 13

"A Question Mark"
Read 2 Corinthians 6:3

Don't put it off; don't frustrate God's work
by showing up late, throwing a question
mark over everything we're doing.
2 Corinthians 6:3

Paul knows his limits, but he also knows his gifts.
He has learned, in the school of Christ, what he
can do and what he cannot do. He is determined
that he will not get in the way, not interfere with
what the Spirit does in the lives of those among
whom he lives for Christ's sake.

What are some of the hardships that Paul experienced?

PRAYER: Lord, as I share your love, I want to stay
out of the way, letting your will make its own way.
I would not manipulate others but leave them free
in your presence, not impose my patterns on
them but leave them free to respond originally to
you. *Amen.*

"Having It All"
Read 2 Corinthians 6:4–10

Immersed in tears, yet always filled
with deep joy; living on handouts,
yet enriching many; having nothing,
having it all.

2 Corinthians 6:10

There is nothing, absolutely nothing, that comes into our lives that cannot become a treasured aspect of an exuberant salvation. Nothing diminished Paul; everything enriched him.

How many items of "exuberant salvation" does Paul list?

PRAYER: Help me, dear Lord, to embrace with abandon everything that comes today, letting you transform each detail of experience into salvation. *Amen.*

"Live Openly"
Read 2 Corinthians 6:11–13

I'm speaking as plainly as I can and with
great affection. Open up your lives. Live
openly and expansively!

2 Corinthians 6:13

The Corinthian Christians are blessed with a pastor and teacher (in Paul) who is generous and uncalculating in his ministry, but they are like a collection of narrow-necked bottles over which water is poured. As the waters of life are poured out over them, very little of it gets into them: "Your lives aren't small, but you're living them in a small way."

Are you restricted?

PRAYER: How much of your grace, O Christ, do I exclude by my narrow-hearted ways? How much of your love have I kept out by my suspicious fears? Help me to acquire a trustful, openhearted response to every truth you bring to me. *Amen.*

OCTOBER 16

"Don't Become Partners"
Read 2 Corinthians 6:14–18

Don't become partners with those who
   reject God. How can you make a partnership out of right and wrong? That's
   not partnership; that's war. Is light best
   friends with dark?

2 Corinthians 6:14

We cannot avoid living or working with those
who do not share faith in Christ; we can and must
avoid arrangements that require us to abandon
our primary allegiance to our Lord, or that obscure our basic commitment to love and be loved
by God.

What scripture does Paul quote?

PRAYER: I want to live deeply involved in the
world, Father, but never compromised by it; I
want to be responsive to those around me, but
never shaped by them. I will need your continuous Spirit direction to do it. Grant it in Jesus'
name. Amen.

OCTOBER 17

"Holy Temples"
Read 2 Corinthians 7:1

With promises like this to pull us on, dear
friends, let's make a clean break with
everything that defiles or distracts us,
both within and without. Let's make our
entire lives fit and holy temples for the
worship of God.

2 Corinthians 7:1

Holiness is not fussy moralism; it is not pious
churchliness. It is wholeness—robust, virile, immense health of body and spirit. The call to holiness is the call to live deeply in the splendor and
brilliance of God's design.

What is your understanding of holiness?

PRAYER: Where did I get all these petty, cautious,
cramped ideas of holiness, Almighty God? Not
from you: you reveal it as all glory and adoration.
Don't let me ever pawn this vision for some shabby
and second-rate substitute, but always be in training and in expectation for the best you have for me
in Christ. *Amen.*

OCTOBER 18

"With You All the Way"
Read 2 Corinthians 7:2–4

Don't think I'm finding fault with you.
I told you earlier that I'm with you all
the way, no matter what.

2 Corinthians 7:3

In the tangle of misunderstanding, which in one way or another must be struggled through in any close relationship, Paul never loses his confidence in what Christ is doing both in the Corinthians and in him. In the face of suspicion and criticism, he continues affirmative and expectant.

Compare this with chapter 6, verse 11.

PRAYER: Compared with Paul, Lord, I am far too easily hurt and discouraged: criticism devastates me; rejection unhinges me. If, like Paul, I cared most for what you commanded, I would be both joyful and steady. Guide me into such mature growth in Christ. *Amen.*

"The Arrival of Titus"
Read 2 Corinthians 7:5–7

Then the God who lifts up the downcast
   lifted our heads and our hearts with the
   arrival of Titus.

2 Corinthians 7:6

God uses us to help each other. Paul recalls a time when he was at his worst and God visited him in the person of Titus, who in turn had been strengthened for just such a work by the Corinthians. The chain of comfort is unending; the cause-effect sequence of love goes on and on.

Whose visit has comforted you?

PRAYER: Why do I think, God, that grown-up Christians do it all by themselves? Paul, the epitome of maturity, required the assistance of Titus, and Titus the assistance of the Corinthians. Whose help do I need? *Amen.*

"You Were Jarred"
Read 2 Corinthians 7:8–13

> Now I'm glad—not that you were upset,
>   but that you were jarred into turning
>   things around. You let the distress bring
>   you to God, not drive you from him.
>   The result was all gain, no loss.
>
> 2 Corinthians 7:9

Paul's earlier letter had contained a painfully sharp rebuke. Were some now accusing him of harsh unconcern? Well, writes Paul, look at the results. When a rebuke is delivered and received as God's word, only good comes from it. This rebuke did not diminish but enhanced all concerned.

What well-timed and well-administered rebuke has spurred you on?

PRAYER: Merciful Lord, I want to be able to accept austerity in the midst of tenderness, and share tenderness in the midst of austerity—whatever is required and at the time it is required—and so become all you intend in your great salvation. *Amen.*

"Confident and Proud"
Read 2 Corinthians 7:14–16

> And I couldn't be more pleased—I'm so
> confident and proud of you.
>
> 2 Corinthians 7:16

How was Paul able to sustain his unshakable confidence in people who were fickle, captious, and contentious? Certainly not by what he knew of them; rather, by what he knew of God's working in them for their eternal salvation.

How many times does Paul assert his confidence in this chapter?

PRAYER: Will you teach me to look at the people around me this way, Lord? To see, first of all and last of all, your will being worked in them, and not to be put off by their inconsistent and uneven faith. *Amen.*

"Totally Spontaneous"

Read 2 Corinthians 8:1–5

This was totally spontaneous, entirely their
own idea, and caught us completely off
guard. What explains it was that they
had first given themselves unreservedly
to God and to us.

2 Corinthians 8:5

Poverty plus joy equals wealth: not only spiritually but economically. The recent offering by the
Greek churches for the "relief of the saints" in
Jerusalem exceeded Paul's expectations because
he had been thinking about how little money they
had, forgetting how much blessing there was to
be shared.

What does this tell you about your own use of
money?

PRAYER: I refuse, Lord, to let anyone put a price
tag on my faith. But I refuse also to let any of my
money be separated from your command. Show
me how to use it and to whom to give it, joyously
and liberally. *Amen.*

"Do Your Best"
Read 2 Corinthians 8:6–7

You do so well in so many things—you
trust God, you're articulate, you're
insightful, you're passionate, you love
us—now, do your best in this, too.

2 Corinthians 8:7

Christians are artists who work with everyday life
as sculptors work with stone, poets with words,
and musicians with sounds. No imitation will satisfy an artist, no mediocrity is tolerable. Always
there is a drive to excel.

How many items of excellence are listed?

PRAYER: Almighty and gracious God, you call me
to the dignity and glory of a life that brings love
into being, experienced and visible. Show me
how to use all my words and all my acts, skillfully
and precisely, as I share your creative work in this
"far better way" (1 Corinthians 12:31). Amen.

OCTOBER 24

"He Became Poor"
Read 2 Corinthians 8:8–9

You are familiar with the generosity of our
Master, Jesus Christ. Rich as he was, he
gave it all away for us—in one stroke he
became poor and we became rich.

2 Corinthians 8:9

We do not become like our Lord by holding on
tightly to whatever we have, but by loosening our
grip and using all money and material as a means
of love. Distribution, not accumulation, is the
mode of grace. Christian living begins by receiving from Christ; it continues by learning to live
like him.

What do you think of poverty?

PRAYER: "Poor" is not an attractive word to me,
Lord. I associate it with problems to be remedied,
not blessings to be embraced. Help me to learn
the Word's gospel definition and discover in my
life the blessings that accompany it. *Amen.*

"Do What You Can"
Read 2 Corinthians 8:10–15

> You've got what it takes to finish it up, so
> go to it. Once the commitment is clear,
> you do what you can, not what you
> can't.
>
> 2 Corinthians 8:11

To become a completed act, a good intention re-
quires a responsible plan. There is no lack, in this
world, of feelings of compassion, but many of the
feelings never get connected to an action that
turns them into facts.

What scripture does Paul quote?

PRAYER: Lord Jesus Christ, I put aside all distractions right now and attend to this person for
whom I care: take my desires for this person's good
and help me to prepare a plan for an action that
will carry out what I intend. Here is my plan. . . .
Accompany me now to its completion, by your
Holy Spirit. Amen.

"Someone Very Popular"
Read 2 Corinthians 8:16–19

We're sending a companion along with
  him, someone very popular in the
  churches for his preaching of the
  Message.

2 Corinthians 8:18

We are curious about this person accompanying
Titus. We would love to know his name. How
many people there must be who engage in faithful ministries that support and sustain us, and
whose "famous" names we will never know!

Do you have any ideas about who this person
was?

PRAYER: How many times, Lord, have I been helped
by people I will never meet, whose names I will
never know? The network of anonymous servants
must be immense. I cannot thank them, but I can
thank you for them. *Amen.*

"Careful in Our Reputation"
Read 2 Corinthians 8:20–22

We're being as careful in our reputation
with the public as in our reputation
with God.

2 Corinthians 8:21

Paul is most careful in his choice of associates in this matter of collecting money for the famine-struck Christians in Jerusalem, so that everyone is assured that the money really will get to the people for whom it was given.

Have you ever been disappointed in how your offerings were used?

PRAYER: I thank you, Lord, for the many, many responsible servants in the church who minister selflessly and honestly, who are "careful in their reputation with the public." With their help, so much more good is done, so much more compassion shared, than I could ever manage by myself. *Amen.*

"Show Them What You're Made Of"
Read 2 Corinthians 8:23–24

Show them what you're made of, the love
I've been talking up in the churches.
Let them see it for themselves!
2 Corinthians 8:24

Titus and the brethren, sent to the Corinthian congregation to receive the offering of money, are thoroughly trustworthy. They must not be received or treated inhospitably, or resentfully: they are not bill collectors; they are partners in witnessing to Christ's love.

Who helps you love your neighbor?

PRAYER: God, when your servants come to me to represent your call to help, to give, to assist, to aid, I hope that I will never treat them rudely but always welcome them courteously, glad to have them as partners in loving my neighbor. *Amen.*

"You're on Board"
Read 2 Corinthians 9:1–5

I know you're on board and ready to
go. I've been bragging about you all
through Macedonia province, telling
them, "Achaia province has been ready
to go on this since last year." Your enthusiasm by now has spread to most of
them.

2 Corinthians 9:2

There is a tension here between confidence and
concern: Paul is convinced that the Corinthians are
enthusiastic and generous in their love and giving;
he also knows that the best of us procrastinate, forget, vacillate. So he takes nothing for granted: he
assumes the best but guards against the worst.

What exactly is Paul worried about?

PRAYER: You know, Father, how often I promise
and don't follow through, zealously commit myself and then drift off apathetically. Then I need
friends and leaders to remind me of my commit-
ments and urge my readiness—and you provide
them. Thank you. *Amen.*

OCTOBER 30

"When the Giver Delights"
Read 2 Corinthians 9:6–8

I want each of you to take plenty of time
    to think it over, and make up your mind
    what you will give. That will protect
    you against sob storics and arm-twisting.
    God loves it when the giver delights in
    the giving.

2 Corinthians 9:7

Offerings are not taxes. Offerings are not bills. Offerings are gifts, cheerfully presented before the God who gives us life. God plants them in the field of the world as seeds that will sprout a harvest of neighbor love.

Do you make your offerings reluctantly or cheerfully?

PRAYER: Almighty God, be Lord of my money: I offer it to you, all of it. Not just a few dollars; not just a portion. Under your lordship, train me in using it cheerfully and bountifully, for the sake of Jesus Christ. *Amen.*

"Bountiful Thanksgivings"
Read 2 Corinthians 9:9–12

Carrying out this social relief work involves
far more than helping meet the bare
needs of poor Christians. It also produces
abundant and bountiful thanksgivings
to God.

2 Corinthians 9:12

Economics, named by some "the dismal science,"
is for the Christian a most happy enterprise. God's
example and command convert it from anxiety-
ridden avarice to free and generous thanksgiving.

What scripture is quoted?

PRAYER: God, free me from stinginess and release
me from the clutches of miserliness. You have
shown me the generous way; you have demonstrated the gladness of the giver contrasted to the
grim and pinched spirit of the covetous. Help me
to live what you have commanded and shown, for
Jesus' sake. *Amen.*

"This Gift, His Gift"
Read 2 Corinthians 9:13–15

Thank God for this gift, his gift. No
language can praise it enough!

2 Corinthians 9:15

Two things are set side by side: "God's gift" to us
and the "generous offerings to your needy brothers and sisters." Our contribution can never match
God's gift, but it can be shaped by it, tested by it,
and enlarged by it. When our lives flow toward
others in the way our Lord's life flows into ours,
we are living well.

Are you living what Paul is here teaching?

PRAYER: I glorify you, great God: in the money I
contribute, in the service I render, in the love I express, in the compassion I share. Let your inex-
pressible gift get expressed, however inadequately,
in what I give in the name of Jesus Christ. *Amen.*

NOVEMBER 2

"Gentle but Firm Spirit"
Read 2 Corinthians 10:1–4

> And now a personal but most urgent
> matter; I write in the gentle but firm
> spirit of Christ. I hear that I'm being
> painted as cringing and wishy-washy
> when I'm with you, but harsh and
> demanding when at a safe distance
> writing letters.
>
> 2 Corinthians 10:1

It is easy to suppose that because we are engaged
in warfare we must also engage in violence, forc-
ing people by any means at hand to acknowledge,
agree, submit, believe God. But we are only permitted to fight by "the gentle but firm spirit of
Christ."

What inappropriate means have you used?

PRAYER: God Almighty, train me in using weapons
of the Spirit—speaking the truth in love, praying
in faithful intercession, acting with courteous
compassion—so that I will be an asset, not a lia-
bility, in the good fight of faith. *Amen.*

"Warped Philosophies"
Read 2 Corinthians 10:5–6

> We use our powerful God-tools for smashing warped philosophies, tearing down barriers erected against the truth of God, fitting every loose thought and emotion and impulse into the structure of life shaped by Christ.
>
> 2 Corinthians 10:5

We are separated from God's will by obstacles that are constructed out of willful ignorance and stubborn pride. One of Paul's apostolic assignments was to demolish the arguments and tear down the warped philosophies. He was a master at it, gently and insistently removing the obstacles that keep us from hearing God and responding to God's love.

What are some obstacles in your life?

PRAYER: "Make me a captive, Lord, and then I shall be free; Force me to render up my sword, And I shall conqueror be" (George Matheson, "Make Me a Captive, Lord," *The Hymnbook*, 308). *Amen.*

"Purpose of Building You Up"
Read 2 Corinthians 10:7–12

You may think I overstate the authority he
gave me, but I'm not backing off. Every
bit of my commitment is for the purpose of building you up, after all, not
tearing you down.

2 Corinthians 10:8

No good comes from comparing leaders, measur-
ing one against another. God has given a variety of
leadership gifts: our task is to accept what is right
for us. The temptation is to shop around for a
glamorous leader who will flatter us, but what we
need is a faithful pastor who will build us up.

What were the Corinthians doing?

PRAYER: I want to experience, Lord Jesus, everything you have for me, the hard disciplines as well
as the sunny blessings, rebukes to my willfulness
along with affirmations of my trust in you, receiving your entire truth in my whole being. *Amen.*

"Sticking to the Limits"
Read 2 Corinthians 10:13–17

We aren't making outrageous claims
here. We're sticking to the limits of
what God has set for us. But there can
be no question that those limits reach
to and include you.

2 Corinthians 10:13

Here is a model for both modesty and boldness: a
realization that one person cannot do everything,
and at the same time a drive to make the most of
what is given. I do my best when I find out what
God has apportioned to me, and then persevere in
it undaunted and unashamed.

Compare this with Jeremiah 9:23–24.

PRAYER: God, help me to stick to the one thing
you have given me to do, to be: not wishing I had
somebody else's job or situation or personality,
but using what you have graciously given and
commanded to bring glory to your name. *Amen.*

"The Difference"
Read 2 Corinthians 10:18

What you say about yourself means
nothing in God's work. It's what God
says about you that makes the difference.
2 Corinthians 10:18

Self-administered commendation is unconvincing.
We cannot improve ourselves by pretending that
we are better than we are. To be worth anything, a
commendation must come from someone who
knows us thoroughly and is for us absolutely. And
who knows us and loves us better than our Lord?

Compare this with Psalm 75:4–7.

PRAYER: Lord Jesus Christ, you have work for me
to do and give me gifts and strength to do it.
Stand with me, beside me, behind me: with you
for me, who can be against me. *Amen.*

"Another Jesus"
Read 2 Corinthians 11:1–4

It seems that if someone shows up
preaching quite another Jesus than we
preached—different spirit, different
message—you put up with him quite
nicely. But if you put up with these
big-shot "apostles," why can't you put
up with simple me?

2 Corinthians 11:4

There is one Jesus Christ, but there are different
representations of him. Some of the differences
are useful variations in emphasis, but some are
dangerous distortions of reality. If we are not to be
deceived and led astray, we cannot naively accept
anything that is told us but must test everything
against the standards of our first love.

What distortions of the gospel are you aware of?

PRAYER: Father in heaven, forgive me when I am
inconstant, and unstable, drifting, and dabbling.
Fix my mind and heart on the revelation so clearly
and sacrificially given in Jesus Christ, and keep me
loyal and faithful, by your Holy Spirit. *Amen.*

NOVEMBER 8

"As Good"
Read 2 Corinthians 11:5–6

I'm as good as they are.

2 Corinthians 11:5

Paul will not let himself be put down by those who compare him unfavorably with more glamorous preachers and teachers. He has been given his apostolic ministry by God and he has carried it out. It is no task of his to compete or to compare, but to do his work courageously and faithfully in Christ's name.

Do you compare yourself unfavorably with others?

PRAYER: I want to see myself as I am in your eyes, dear Father, not as I am in the eyes of others. I want to understand myself uniquely, created in your image and redeemed by Christ's blood, not in comparison with someone else. *Amen.*

"Did I Make a Bad Mistake?"
Read 2 Corinthians 11:7–11

I wonder, did I make a bad mistake in
proclaiming God's Message to you
without asking for something in return,
serving you free of charge so that you
wouldn't be inconvenienced by me?
                                    2 Corinthians 11:7

In retrospect, it seems that Paul may have made a
mistake: he bent over backwards when he lived
with them not to be a burden to them, getting his
support from more mature Christians in Philippi
and Thessalonica. But now that these Corinthians
are in a position to help others, they seem reluc-
tant to do it. Do they have no sense of gratitude?
No generous impulse?

Do you think Paul made a mistake in what he
did?

PRAYER: I hope, Lord, that I never take for granted
the sacrifices others make for me or the gifts that
others make available to me. Even if I cannot respond to them directly, I want to live sacrificially
and gratefully for others, so that they may experience your generosity in my actions. *Amen.*

NOVEMBER 10

"Not Changing My Position"
Read 2 Corinthians 11:12

And I'm not changing my position on this.
I'd die before taking your money. I'm
giving nobody grounds for lumping me
in with those money-grubbing "preachers," vaunting themselves as something
special.

2 Corinthians 11:12

Good work is not conditioned by popular vote.
What glorifies God, not what pleases or attracts
people, is the thing worth doing—and the thing
that lasts. The person who continues in faith and
obedience in spite of indifference or opposition
does the best work.

Do you ever feel like quitting?

PRAYER: Keep me, Father, steady and persevering,
carrying out the tasks I find assigned to me, using
the gifts that are given to me. Keep me from dis-
couragement or envy. Equip me with daily strength
and sufficient hope. *Amen.*

NOVEMBER 11

"Satan Does It All the Time"
Read 2 Corinthians 11:13–15

And no wonder! Satan does it all the time,
dressing up as a beautiful angel of light.
2 Corinthians 11:14

Because the appearance of people who preach and
teach can easily mislead us, the substance of their
message and their lives must be examined. Many
use the forms of Christian ministry to gain power
or money or prestige: the problem of deceit is
ever-present; therefore, the necessity for discern-
ment is imperative.

How do you discern "sham to the core"?

PRAYER: Lord, I want to be open to all who teach
truth, but not gullible to everyone who speaks in
a pious voice. I want to be responsive to all who
will lead me in love, but not pliable to anyone
who would influence me by manipulating my
sentiments. In the name of Jesus Christ. *Amen.*

"Accept That I Am a Fool"
Read 2 Corinthians 11:16–17

Let me come back to where I started—and
don't hold it against me if I continue to
sound a little foolish. Or if you'd rather,
just accept that I am a fool and let me
rant on a little.

2 Corinthians 11:16

Self-praise is foolish. Paul knows that it is. But if it
is the only language the Corinthians understand,
he will use it. There is nothing apostolic about
what he is doing, nothing in Jesus' example or
teaching. Paul only does it because he thinks it is
required by the circumstances.

What does Paul mean by "fool"?

PRAYER: "I bow my forehead to the dust, I veil
mine eyes for shame, And urge, in trembling self-
distrust, A prayer without a claim. No offering of
mine own have I, No works my faith to prove; I
can but give the gifts He gave, And plead His love
for love" (John Greenleaf Whittier, "I Bow My
Forehead to the Dust," *The Hymnbook*, 109). *Amen.*

NOVEMBER 13

"Put You Down"
Read 2 Corinthians 11:18–22

You have such admirable tolerance for
impostors who rob your freedom,
rip you off, steal you blind, put you
down—even slap your face!

2 Corinthians 11:20

These people more than tolerate false teachers
who trample all over them: domineering, grasping, crafty, arrogant, violent; and they criticize as
not "strong" one who showed them the greatest
consideration!

What characteristics do you admire in Christian leaders?

PRAYER: God, help me to honor in others the
things that you commend: modesty, quiet humility, diligent faithfulness. And keep me from being
distracted by the pushy self-advertising of those
who merchandise gospel. *Amen.*

"I'm Their Match"
Read 2 Corinthians 11:21–22

Do they brag of being Hebrews, Israelites,
   the pure race of Abraham? I'm their
   match.

2 Corinthians 11:22

The false apostles in Corinth were claiming superiority by virtue of their race and ancestry. But famous grandparents are not qualifying credentials. There is no master race. All of us have a common ancestry if we go back far enough.

What ancestors are you proud of?

PRAYER: I thank you, heavenly Father, for brave and true fathers in the faith. I would be humble before them, not proud of them. Use their lives to challenge and guide me in the way of faith. *Amen.*

"I've Worked Much Harder"
Read 2 Corinthians 11:23–27

Are they servants of Christ? I can go them
one better. (I can't believe I'm saying
these things. It's crazy to talk this way!
But I started, and I'm going to finish.)
I've worked much harder, been jailed
more often, beaten up more times than
I can count, and at death's door time
after time.

2 Corinthians 11:23

His wounds are his credentials: Paul never hesi-
tated to work in Christ's name for fear of pain, or
inconvenience, or calumny. His life is a contrast to
the many who engage in Christian ministry for
what they can get out of it, and when it is no
longer convenient or profitable, abandon it.

How many items does Paul list?

PRAYER: God, you called me to deny myself, take
up my cross daily, and follow you. And I have said
yes to your call: now help me to persevere in my
obedience, enduring to the end. *Amen.*

"The Daily Pressures"
Read 2 Corinthians 11:28–29

And that's not the half of it, when you
throw in the daily pressures and
anxieties of all the churches.

2 Corinthians 11:28

There is high adventure in Paul's life, but there is
daily stress as well. He is a bold missionary, when
that is called for; he is a persevering pastor, when
that is necessary. He accepts the pain of persecution from outsiders and the anxiety of high-stress
relationships in the churches, avoiding neither,
embracing both.

What kind of pressure came from the churches?

PRAYER: Prepare me for the tasks ahead, Lord Jesus:
whether it be a sudden crisis to which I must respond with courage or a long routine that I must
face with patience. Help me never to shrink from
the tough challenges nor shirk the everyday pressures, but to accept both in the name of the Lord
Jesus. *Amen.*

"I'm Not Lying"
Read 2 Corinthians 11:30–31

The eternal and blessed God and Father of
our Master Jesus knows I'm not lying.
                                    2 Corinthians 11:31

Will some remain skeptical of the sincerity or
good sense of this person who openly shares his
weaknesses and refuses to parade his achievements? But in this he is only following the example of his Lord. Under God, who gave Jesus "the
status of a slave" (Philippians 2:7), this should
not seem at all unusual but the normal pattern of
Christian witness.

Compare this with Philippians 2:1–22.

PRAYER: I look to Jesus, great God, for my example. After the manner of him who came not to be
served but to serve, I want to walk in the way of
humility and charity, giving freely both what I
have and who I am, in Jesus' name. *Amen.*

"In Damascus"

Read 2 Corinthians 11:32–33

Remember the time I was in Damascus
  and the governor of King Aretas posted
  guards at the city gates to arrest me?

2 Corinthians 11:32

Paul set out for Damascus as a persecutor of Christians; he left it being persecuted as a Christian. The city was where his life was transformed so that he no longer zealously did God's work for Him but submissively let God's work be done in him.

What else happened in Damascus?

PRAYER: I thank you, Lord God, for the deep changes you bring about in me by the visitations of your Holy Spirit. As I remember the places where I have been surprised by your grace and blessed by your salvation, I praise you, in Jesus' name. *Amen.*

NOVEMBER 19

"Visions and Revelations"
Read 2 Corinthians 12:1–6

You've forced me to talk this way, and I do
it against my better judgment. But now
that we're at it, I may as well bring up
the matter of visions and revelations that
God gave me.

2 Corinthians 12:1

There were imprisonments and shipwrecks; there
were also visions and revelations. If the life of
faith experiences hard and painful rejections, it
also experiences intense and deep ecstasies.

Whom is Paul talking about?

PRAYER: "We would see Jesus; in the early morn-
ing Still as of old He calleth, 'Follow Me'; Let us
arise, all meaner service scorning: Lord we are
Thine, we give ourselves to Thee!" (J. Edgar Park,
"We Would See Jesus; Lo! His Star Is Shining," *The
Hymnbook*, 183). *Amen.*

NOVEMBER 20

"A Handicap"
Read 2 Corinthians 12:7–9

Because of the extravagance of those revelations, and so I wouldn't get a big
head, I was given the gift of a handicap
to keep me in constant touch with my
limitations.

2 Corinthians 12:7

Pain can be a goad to prayer; the realization of inadequacy can be the means to experiencing the
sufficiency of grace. Weakness is a breach in the
thick walls of self-righteous pride that gives fresh
access to Christ's power.

What "handicap" have you had?

PRAYER: I praise you for sufficient grace, all-pow-
erful Christ: I thank you for the weakness that
forces me to rely on your strength, for the pain
that makes me seek your comfort, for every ha-
rassment that drives me to live by your peace.
Amen.

"I Take Limitations in Stride"
Read 2 Corinthians 12:10

Now I take limitations in stride, and with
good cheer, these limitations that cut
me down to size—abuse, accidents,
opposition, bad breaks. I just let Christ
take over! And so the weaker I get, the
stronger I become.

2 Corinthians 12:10

We do not develop a life of faith by building defense systems against calamity. Weaknesses are not liabilities that we are ashamed of, but the very conditions in which we experience the action of Christ in us.

What are your weaknesses?

PRAYER: Instead of hiding my weaknesses, and trying to avoid calamities, O God, I will accept and face them both: the inadequacies within, the difficulties without. For it is not by my power nor by my righteousness that salvation comes, but by your power and righteousness in Christ, in whose name I pray. Amen.

"A True Apostle"
Read 2 Corinthians 12:11–13

All the signs that mark a true apostle were
in evidence while I was with you through
both good times and bad: signs of por-
tent, signs of wonder, signs of power.

2 Corinthians 12:12

Paul, persistent and faithful in his ministry, was
compared (unfavorably!) with fly-by-night "big-
shot apostles" who made a dazzling impression
but never shared the sufferings or the disciplines
or the responsibilities of a spirit-led community.

What were the marks of Paul's authenticity?

PRAYER: Lord Jesus Christ, deepen my appreciation for your servants who bring your word to me
truly, who share their lives with me generously,
and who work with me faithfully. *Amen.*

"Only in You"
Read 2 Corinthians 12:14–15

Everything is in readiness now for this, my
third visit to you. But don't worry about
it; you won't have to put yourselves out.
I'll be no more of a bother to you this
time than on the other visits. I have no
interest in what you have—only in you.
Children shouldn't have to look out for
their parents; parents look out for the
children.

2 Corinthians 12:14

In spite of the prevalence of religious teachers who
"used" congregations to their own advantage, that
accusation is not credible in relation to Paul. He insists on being judged by the Corinthian Christians'
firsthand knowledge of him, and not by insinua-
tions made about him.

What was the accusation against Paul?

PRAYER: Heavenly Father, develop in me a sense of
generosity to others, so that I will always see them
as people to love, not as tools to use, and appreciate them as your children, not as people whom I
can manipulate to my advantage. Amen.

"Where's the Evidence?"
Read 2 Corinthians 12:16–18

> Where's the evidence? Did I cheat or trick
>   you through anyone I sent?
>
> 2 Corinthians 12:17

There is impressive, painstaking work being done
here: every suspicion is dealt with, every accusation met, every innuendo made explicit and answered. Paul cannot be too careful, for it is the
credibility of the gospel, not his own reputation,
that is at stake.

Compare this with chapter 8, verses 22–23.

PRAYER: I am grateful, Lord, for the countless ways
in which you take me seriously, dealing with my
petty objections and criticisms, my narrow ignorance and small-minded prejudices. As a result of
your patience, I am gradually learning to live in a
wider world of trust and love and hope. *Amen.*

"Of Your Growing Up"
Read 2 Corinthians 12:19 -21

> I hope you don't think that all along we've
>   been making our defense before you,
>   the jury. You're not the jury; God is the
>   jury—God revealed in Christ— and we
>   make our case before him. And we've
>   gone to all the trouble of supporting
>   ourselves so that we won't be in the way
>   or get in the way of your growing up.
>   2 Corinthians 12:19

The correspondence between Paul and the Corinthians could easily have degenerated into an exchange of recriminations. What it is, in fact, is a remarkable case study in reconciliation. Why? Because in the complex tangle of feelings and arguments, Paul never for a moment lost sight of his goal: their "growing up."

How many specific fears does Paul name?

PRAYER: God of mercy, train me in the gospel skills that know how to use misunderstandings and criticisms to develop a community of reconciliation, so that my differences with others do not become quarrels, but ways of experiencing generous forgiveness and appreciative love. *Amen.*

"A Matter Becomes Clear"
Read 2 Corinthians 13:1

Well, this is my third visit coming up.
    Remember the Scripture that says, "A
    matter becomes clear after two or three
    witnesses give evidence"?

2 Corinthians 13:1

In the community of faith, confrontations are allowed, even encouraged. But we are not permitted to indulge in hearsay and bickering. The church is the proper place to settle conflicts; it is not the place to indulge in scurrilous gossip or sullen bickering.

Read the biblical guidance on this matter in Deuteronomy 19:15.

PRAYER: God, I want to be honest and open when I feel myself to be in conflict with others: show me how to use our differences to achieve a harmony, not as excuses to pick a fight, for Jesus' sake. Amen.

"The Full Force"
Read 2 Corinthians 13:2–4

You who have been demanding proof that
  Christ speaks through me will get more
  than you bargained for. You'll get the
  full force of Christ, don't think you
  won't.

2 Corinthians 13:3

Gentleness must not be confused with weakness.
Mercy must not be equated with softness. An immense power develops out of the apparent weakness of the crucified, and it disciplines sin. No sin
is condoned; no laxness is spared.

Compare this with Philippians 2:7–8.

PRAYER: "Give we the glory and praise to the Lamb;
Take we the robe and the harp and the palm; Sing
we the son of the Lamb that was slain, Dying in
weakness, but rising to reign" (Horatius Bonar,
"Blessing and Honor and Glory and Power," *The
Hymnbook*, 137). *Amen.*

"Test Yourselves"
Read 2 Corinthians 13:5–6

Test yourselves to make sure you are solid
in the faith. Don't drift along taking
everything for granted. Give yourselves
regular checkups. You need firsthand
evidence, not mere hearsay, that Jesus
Christ is in you. Test it out. If you fail
the test, do something about it.

2 Corinthians 13:5

Our self-examination must be dominated by the
realization that Christ is in us. It must not become
nit-picking introspection or morbid scrupulosity.
Our inner lives are, more than anything else, the
environment in which Christ makes his home.

Do you make a habit of examining yourself?

PRAYER: "Investigate my life, O God, find out
everything about me; Cross-examine and test me,
get a clear picture of what I'm about; See for
yourself whether I've done anything wrong—
then guide me on the road to eternal life" (Psalm
139:23–24). *Amen.*

"Come Together"
Read 2 Corinthians 13:7–9

We don't just put up with our limitations;
we celebrate them, and then go on to
celebrate every strength, every triumph
of the truth in you. We pray hard that it
will all come together in your lives.

2 Corinthians 13:9

How fortunate these people were to have Paul
writing to them and praying for them: in him
they have a wise, skilled guide in the life of Christ.
They don't have a critic looking over their shoulder, accusing and blaming them when they fail in
the test; they have an advocate, an ally, a friend.

Who has contributed to your improvement?

PRAYER: God, I want to do this same thing for others: help them through the difficult days, pray
them through the hard times, counsel them
through the confused circumstances, so that they
may never lose touch with grace and peace and always grow in the confidence that you are for them
in Jesus. *Amen.*

"Putting People Together"
Read 2 Corinthians 13:10

I'm writing this to you now so that when
I come I won't have to say another word
on the subject. The authority the Master
gave me is for putting people together,
not taking them apart. I want to get on
with it, and not have to spend time on
reprimands.

2 Corinthians 13:10

The note of severity can be sounded if necessary:
it is far better if Christians will spontaneously listen, repent, love, and praise. But some kinds of
stubbornness and rebellion, especially in the very
immature, or in the habitually self-indulgent, require the severe discipline of correction.

How are you being built up?

PRAYER: Build this temple of your Spirit, O Lord,
along lines that are straight and on foundations
that are firm. I want my life to be spacious, hospitable to your visitations and open to friends and
strangers. *Amen.*

DECEMBER 1

"That's About It"
Read 2 Corinthians 13:11–13

And that's about it, friends. Be cheerful.
  Keep things in good repair. Keep your
  spirits up. Think in harmony. Be agree-
  able. Do all that, and the God of love
  and peace will be with you for sure.
                        2 Corinthians 13:11

Since the life of faith is lived in the laboratory of a
community, care must be experienced as we love
one another and are at peace with each other: affectionate greetings sincerely given and received
are gospel signs.

How do you express your affection?

PRAYER: God, let me find ways to express your
love to and with the people I meet today: directly
and indirectly, in spontaneous affection and careful strategies of goodwill, so that what you will
for others may find a witness in me. *Amen.*

"Grace . . . Love . . . Friendship"
Read 2 Corinthians 13:14

The amazing grace of the Master, Jesus
Christ, the extravagant love of God, the
intimate friendship of the Holy Spirit,
be with all of you.

2 Corinthians 13:14

Everything we know and experience of God is
compressed into these three phrases: God is for us
in Jesus (grace); God is with us in the Father
(love); God is in us in the Holy Spirit (friendship). It is the glory of the Christian to live, unin-
terruptedly, under this benediction.

What is a benediction?

PRAYER: "God be in my head, And in my understanding; God be in mine eyes, And in my looking; God be in my mouth, And in my speaking;
God be in my heart, And in my thinking; God be
at mine end, And at my departing" (Sarum Primer,
"God Be in My Head," *The Hymnbook*, 395). *Amen.*

"Stalwart Followers of Christ"
Read Colossians 1:1–8

> I, Paul, have been sent on special assign-
> ment by Christ as part of God's master
> plan. Together with my friend Timothy,
> I greet the Christians and stalwart fol-
> lowers of Christ who live in Colosse.
> May everything good from God our
> Father be yours!
>
> *Colossians 1:1–2*

Paul, in his salutation to the Colossian Christians
and his reminders of the Message's truth for them,
is sure of himself and sure of the Colossian community. His confidence is based on what he knows
himself to be by the will of God and what he
knows the Colossians are by their faith in Jesus
Christ.

What are you most sure of about God?

PRAYER: I thank you, Lord, for calling me into
being by your grace, for providing for my salvation in Jesus Christ, and for now setting me in relationships of love and peace and hope. *Amen.*

DECEMBER 4

"As You Learn More and More"
Read Colossians 1:9–12

We pray that you'll live well for the Master,
making him proud of you as you work
hard in his orchard. As you learn more
and more how God works, you will
learn how to do your work.

Colossians 1:10

Life in Christ is a country to walk in, not a panorama to look at. We must not remain at the edges, content with mere glimpses. Each step of faith brings us into range of a better hope, into encounter with a deeper love. On the path of pilgrimage nothing diminishes or becomes stale, everything increases and freshens.

What is new for you in the life of faith?

PRAYER: "Light up Thy Word; the fettered page From killing bondage free: Light up our way; lead forth this age In love's large liberty. O Light of light! within us dwell, Through us Thy radiance pour, That word and life Thy truths may tell, And praise Thee evermore" (Washington Gladden, "O Lord of Life, to Thee We Lift," *The Hymnbook*, 256). *Amen.*

DECEMBER 5

"Supreme"

Read Colossians 1:13–18

He was supreme in the beginning and—
   leading the resurrection parade—he is
   supreme in the end.

Colossians 1:18

Jesus Christ is the beginning point for all experience and knowledge of God. But he is not a beginning that we leave behind as we acquire more knowledge and experience. He is also the end. We do not graduate from him, we grow in and with him.

What similarities do you see between this and John's treatment of a similar theme in John 1:14–18?

PRAYER: Gather, O God, the dissociated experiences I have of eternal life and put them all together for me in Jesus Christ, who is both center and circumference for me. *Amen.*

"Spacious"

Read Colossians 1:19–20

> So spacious is he, so roomy, that everything
> of God finds its proper place in him
> without crowding.
>
> *Colossians 1:19*

We meet life in the form of fragments, broken pieces scattered in disorder. Christ establishes a sense of plenitude. The world is full to overflowing, and it all connects even though its mysteries will never be dissipated.

How does God accomplish wholeness?

PRAYER: Lord Jesus Christ, I lay before you the bits and pieces of my life, such as they are. I can make no sense out of them. I can fashion no order among them. Take my offering and make a new creature: I want to share your wholeness and live by your reconciliation, at peace with earth and heaven. *Amen.*

"Your Backs Turned to God"

Read Colossians 1:21–23

> You yourselves are a case study of what
>   he does. At one time you all had your
>   backs turned to God, thinking rebellious
>   thoughts of him, giving him trouble
>   every chance you got.
>
> Colossians 1:21

"Rebellious thoughts" and "giving him trouble" are contrasted with "grounded" and "steady." One way of life expresses all the disorder caused by sin; the other way witnesses to the coherence wrought by the cross.

Why does God reconcile us?

PRAYER: Keep the alternatives plain before me, O God: the way life degenerates into chaos and futility when I assert my own pride; the way life develops wholeness and meaning when I stay "tuned in to the Message." And keep me faithful, being "careful not to be distracted or diverted." For Jesus' sake. *Amen.*

DECEMBER 8

"Out in the Open"
Read Colossians 1:24–26

> This mystery has been kept in the dark
> for a long time, but now it's out in the
> open.
>
> Colossians 1:26

Ingenious attempts to penetrate the mystery of
God and salvation—centuries of mythmaking and
mathematics—had come no nearer the truth; and
then in a stroke it was all out in the open, the
secret told, plainly and publicly in Jesus Christ.
The thousands of stars that flickered in the night
of pagan cults now gave way to the one Sun proclaimed in the apostles' gospel.

Why was Paul "a servant in this church"?

PRAYER: I thank you, O God, that my life is not
lived in a thick fog, dark with mystery and omi-
nous with shadows, but in the clear light of your
revealed love for me in Jesus. In whose name I
pray. Amen.

"To Be Mature"
Read Colossians 1:27–29

We teach in a spirit of profound common
sense so that we can bring each person
to maturity. To be mature is to be basic.
Christ! No more, no less.

Colossians 1:28

The base of maturity is "Christ is in you"; its apex
is "sharing in God's glory." Maturity is the wholeness that comes when we recognize God's fullness
in Christ, and then receive it into ourselves by
grace. Both what God is and what we may become
are in the Christ.

What is Paul's aim as a minister?

PRAYER: "Fountain of o'erflowing grace, Freely
from Thy fullness give; Till I close my earthly race,
May I prove it Christ to live" (Ralph Wardlaw,
"Christ of All My Hopes the Ground," *The Hymnbook*, 314). *Amen.*

"A Tapestry of Love"
Read Colossians 2:1–5

I want you woven into a tapestry of love,
in touch with everything there is to
know of God. Then you will have minds
confident and at rest, focused on Christ,
God's great mystery.

Colossians 2:2

The knowledge that comes from Christ does not make us smarter than our neighbor so that we can have secrets from him or assert a superiority over her; rather, it provides insights into God's ways in our neighbor so that we are drawn closer to him or her. The result is that, instead of being divided into factions, we are woven into a tapestry of a loving community.

What in the Colossian church pleases Paul?

PRAYER: O God, grant that my knowledge may never become abstract, nor my love depersonalized. I want the kind of knowledge that brings me into a better understanding of your ways and motivates me to share what you are doing in the world. *Amen.*

DECEMBER 11

"Rooted in Him"
Read Colossians 2:6–7

> You received Christ Jesus, the Master; now
> live in him. You're deeply rooted in him.
> You're well constructed upon him. You
> know your way around the faith. Now
> do what you've been taught. School's
> out; quit studying the subject and start
> living it! And let your living spill over
> into thanksgiving.
>
> *Colossians 2:7*

All life needs basis. We need a place to stand, a ground for our being. Jesus Christ is soil in which to take root and a foundation upon which to build.

Recall the parable of the soils (Mark 4:1–9) in relation to this.

PRAYER: Lord Jesus Christ, I want your life established in my bloodstream and nervous system, my breathing and my talking, my walking and my working. I don't want any of it left on the outside as something to be admired or discussed; I want it all inside where it becomes part of me, received in faith and expressed in thanksgiving. *Amen.*

"Big Words"
Read Colossians 2:8–12

Watch out for people who try to dazzle
you with big words and intellectual
double-talk. They want to drag you
off into endless arguments that never
amount to anything. They spread their
ideas through the empty traditions of
human beings and the empty superstitions of spirit beings. But that's not
the way of Christ.

Colossians 2:8

The believers in Colosse had been unsettled by
teachers who made a great show of learning and
taught a complicated religion full of intriguing
mysteries and intricate myths. It was mostly hot
air. Paul demonstrated its emptiness and proclaimed the fullness of life in Christ.

Do you know any present-day instances of
"empty superstitions"?

PRAYER: God, fill my mind with thoughts of you,
my heart with love for you, and my body with
obedience to you so that there is neither room nor
time for anything else: "Animate my trivial days
and ram them with the sun" (William B. Yeats).
Amen.

DECEMBER 13

"Their Sham Authority"
Read Colossians 2:13–15

He stripped all the spiritual tyrants in the
universe of their sham authority at the
Cross and marched them naked through
the streets.

Colossians 2:15

One of the great achievements of the gospel is that
it puts evil in its place. The gospel does not deny
the existence of evil—there are malign powers in
the world ("spiritual tyrants"). It does not deny
that they have a certain influence. They are a danger to be wary of, not a threat to be appeased.
"The prince of darkness grim, We tremble not for
him" (Martin Luther, "A Mighty Fortress Is Our
God").

What evil are you no longer afraid of?

PRAYER: Your victory, O Christ, was decisive over
evil at the cross: let no superstition or anxiety re-
vive its old influence in my heart. Let faith, not
fear, be at the core of my being this day. *Amen.*

"The Substance Is Christ"

Read Colossians 2:16–19

All those things are mere shadows cast
before what was to come; the substance
is Christ.

Colossians 2:17

Human observances, even when they are religious observances, do not make up a gospel. They are useful only insofar as they hint at and point toward the realities of the God who has revealed himself in Jesus Christ.

Who is "the Head"?

PRAYER: I affirm the substance, not the shadows, O God: the solid realities of what you do in Jesus Christ, not the flickering imaginations of humanity's guesses about you. "On Christ, the solid Rock, I stand; All other ground is sinking sand" (Edward Mote, "My Hope Is Built on Nothing Less," *The Hymnbook*, 368). *Amen.*

DECEMBER 15

"Don't Touch This!"
Read Colossians 2:20–23

So, then, if with Christ you've put all that
pretentious and infantile religion behind
you, why do you let yourselves be bul-
lied by it? "Don't touch this! Don't taste
that! Don't go near this!"

Colossians 2:20–21

In the pagan world, demons were believed to lurk
in some foods and in certain places. A system of
taboos kept the people from unwittingly falling
under the malign powers. Then the gospel proclaimed a general exorcism: Christ banished the
demons. Consequently, all foods were clean and all
places safe. Taboos were replaced by the cheerful
command, "So, eat your meals heartily, not worrying about what others say about you—you're
eating to God's glory" (1 Corinthians 10:31).

Do you have any secret superstitions?

PRAYER: Thank you, O Christ, for showing me
how everything material bears the signature of
your creative power. In all that I touch and handle
and taste this day, increase a loving appreciation in
me for what you have provided. *Amen.*

DECEMBER 16

"Pursue"

Read Colossians 3:1–4

So if you're serious about living this new
resurrection life with Christ, *act* like it.
Pursue the things over which Christ
presides.

Colossians 3:1

The resurrection of Jesus Christ is the pivot upon
which all God's purposes turn. It is also the hidden center of our lives: every motive and every
goal find their origin and definition in the resurrection.

What practical consequences does the resurrection have for you?

PRAYER: "Christ of the Upward Way, My Guide
divine, Where Thou hast set Thy feet May I place
mine; And move and march wherever Thou hast
trod, Keeping face forward up the hill of God"
(Walter J. Mathams, "Christ of the Upward Way,"
The Hymnbook, 295). Amen.

DECEMBER 17

"Everyone Is Included"
Read Colossians 3:5–11

Words like Jewish and non-Jewish,
     religious and irreligious, insider and
     outsider, uncivilized and uncouth,
     slave and free, mean nothing. From
     now on everyone is defined by Christ,
     everyone is included in Christ.

Colossians 3:11

Sin uses every natural difference among us—differences of race, of culture, of social class—as a wedge to divide us. Christ uses the same differences to arrange a community. He doesn't do it by making us all look and talk alike, but by becoming a center around which our differences are a harmony.

How many vices does Paul list?

PRAYER: Old habits, Lord, keep intruding into my life. I put up barriers and make defenses. I wall myself off from those you have sent to be my friends and companions. Help me to put aside every anxious defense and live openly and intimately in the spirit of Christ. *Amen.*

"As the Master Forgave You"
Read Colossians 3:12–15

Be even-tempered, content with second
place, quick to forgive an offense.
Forgive as quickly and completely as
the Master forgave you.

Colossians 3:13

The word "forgiveness" has been watered down
by journalistic cant and careless usage. For many,
it is the verbal equivalent of a shoulder shrug.
When, though, we discover its impact and realize
its meaning in Christ on the cross, we find that it
is the most creative act in which we can engage.

How does the cross of Christ deepen your understanding of forgiveness?

PRAYER: You know, Lord, all the ways I have of
treating people I don't like: I judge them, I avoid
them, I gossip about them, I hector them. But I
don't want to do it anymore: I want to learn to
forgive, even as you have forgiven me, in Jesus
Christ. *Amen.*

"Every Detail"
Read Colossians 3:16–17

Let every detail in your lives—words,
actions, whatever—be done in the name
of the Master, Jesus, thanking God the
Father every step of the way.

Colossians 3:17

When Christians gather together, vibrations of thankfulness create internal rhythms of praise. The conversation is lively, the songs animated, and the community spirit congenial. The liveliness and the unity are created by the all-encompassing and all-enlivening word of Christ.

What "singing your hearts out to God" do you enjoy the most?

PRAYER: "Morning has broken Like the first morning, Blackbird has spoken like the first bird. Praise for the singing! Praise for the morning! Praise for them, springing Fresh from the Word!" (Eleanor Farjeon, "Morning Has Broken," *The Hymnbook*, 464). *Amen.*

"Work from the Heart"
Read Colossians 3:18–4:1

Work from the heart for your real Master,
for God, confident that you'll get paid
in full when you come into your inheritance. Keep in mind always that the
ultimate Master you're serving is Christ.
Colossians 3:23–24

Christ revolutionizes not only our relationship
with God but every human relationship as well,
whether marital, family, work, or social. Having
put us right with God, he goes on to guide us in
our actions and attitudes toward one another.

In what human relationships do you most need
God's help?

PRAYER: O God, just as you have made things right
between me and you, so make them right between
me and those with whom I live today: the mem-
bers of my family, the people I work with, friends
and strangers I will meet. Enable me to live wisely
and lovingly with them all, in the name of Jesus
Christ. *Amen.*

"Locked Up in This Jail"
Read Colossians 4:2–4

Pray diligently. Stay alert, with your eyes
wide open in gratitude. Don't forget to
pray for us, that God will open doors for
telling the mystery of Christ, even while
I'm locked up in this jail.

Colossians 4:2–3

The present circumstance, whether pleasant or
difficult, was always for Paul a means that God
used to accomplish his purposes. The doors that
closed in on Paul became doors through which
the gospel entered into the lives of many. The
writing and preaching that Paul did in prison
were emancipation for the world that put him
there.

What difficult circumstance in your life is God
using to bring good to another?

PRAYER: How little I understand the sweep of your
purposes, Almighty God, the contrivances of grace
and the ingenuities of love. Take the place I am
now and the limitations imposed on my life and
make them a means for declaring your good news
in Jesus Christ. *Amen.*

"Outsiders"

Read Colossians 4:5–6

Use your heads as you live and work
  among outsiders. Don't miss a trick.
Make the most of every opportunity.

Colossians 4:5

The person outside the faith is not an enemy to be conquered but a brother or sister to be reclaimed. Conduct toward the outsider must be shaped, not with the intent of getting the best of him, but of gaining him for the best; not to show how wrong she is, but to persuade her of the right of Christ.

What outsider are you concerned for?

PRAYER: Use my conduct, O God, to publish your love, to persuade and to convince, so that the evidence of my life may carry conviction with the jury of outsiders who observe me today. *Amen.*

"Trusted Minister and Companion"
Read Colossians 4:7–9

My good friend Tychicus will tell you all
about me. He's a trusted minister and
companion in the service of the Master.
Colossians 4:7

C. S. Lewis wrote: "Friendship . . . is the instrument by which God reveals to each the beauties of all the others . . . they are, like all beauties, derived from Him, and then, in a good friendship, increased by Him through the Friendship itself, so that it is His instrument for creating as well as for revealing." Paul, rich in companions, knew that better than most.

Who are your best friends in the faith?

PRAYER: Give me insight into my friendships, Lord, to see your gifts in them—heightened joys, shared burdens, reflected beauties. And help me to be a good friend to others—faithful and affectionate, loyal and generous. *Amen.*

DECEMBER 24

"Nympha and the Church"
Read Colossians 4:10–17

Say hello to our friends in Laodicea; also to
Nympha and the church that meets in
her house.

Colossians 4:15

Homes were the first cathedrals. When the early
Christians went to church they gathered in the
home of a friend. And even today a church is only
an expanded hearth. The church is a community
of the Holy Spirit; it is also a group of friends who
are known to each other, caringly and affection-
ately.

Where does your church meet?

PRAYER: I want my home, God, to be a center for
witness and friendship. May everyone who comes
into it find it a place where they are accepted and
taken seriously. As they participate in its life, may
they recognize your love shining through the do-
mestic routines. *Amen.*

DECEMBER 25

"In This Jail"
Read Colossians 4:18

I'm signing off in my own handwriting—
Paul. Remember to pray for me in this
jail. Grace be with you.

Colossians 4:18

Paul, who preached liberty in Christ, and whose
ministry was the means by which so many discovered a life free from sin, did some of his most
effective witness and writing with cold steel fet-
ters pressing his flesh.

What effect did imprisonment have on Paul?

PRAYER: Let me not, O Lord, take any joy or blessing in a way that makes me indifferent to or separate from the needs of others. In my freedom, I
would not forget those who are in chains. In my
joy, I would not forget those who are burdened by
anxiety. *Amen.*

"To You, Philemon"

Read Philemon verses 1–3

> I, Paul, am a prisoner for the sake of Christ,
> here with my brother Timothy. I write
> this letter to you, Philemon, my good
> friend and companion in this work.
>
> *Philemon verse 1*

Onesimus, a runaway slave, had come under Paul's influence and had become a Christian. Paul, from his prison cell, sends him back to his master, Philemon, with this letter in hand, a letter of gospel intercession unusually creative in the way it combines matters of justice and mercy with the affairs of everyday life.

Review what you know of the story of Philemon and Onesimus.

PRAYER: Father and Savior God, interrupt my runaway life with mercy. Intervene in my escapist fantasies with grace. Return me to my place of worship and work, for the sake of and in the name of Jesus Christ. *Amen.*

DECEMBER 27

"How Good"

Read Philemon verses 4–7

Friend, you have no idea how good your
    love makes me feel, doubly so when
I see your hospitality to fellow believers.

Philemon verse 7

When Philemon shared his faith, he both talked
about it and acted it out: the same love he had for
God he exhibited to Christian brothers and sisters
("to other Christians"). Such a life is obviously
pleasing to God; it also refreshes those with whom
it is shared.

What reasons does Paul have for being thankful
for Philemon?

PRAYER: Take the love I have for you, dear God,
and show me how to put it to work in the world.
Is there a heavy burden I can help lift? a cheering
word I can speak? a flagging will I can inspire?
You know where the needs are: use me, as you
will, to refresh the saints. *Amen.*

"Useless . . . Useful"
Read Philemon verses 8–14

While here in jail, I've fathered a child, so
to speak. And here he is, hand-carrying
this letter—Onesimus! He was useless
to you before; now he's useful to both
of us.

Philemon verses 10–11

Onesimus has been changed; he has become a
Christian. The slave has become a son. As a runaway slave, he was useless; as a returning son, he
is a valuable addition to the Christian church that
meets in Philemon's house.

What is Paul's attitude to Onesimus?

PRAYER: Lord, I want to see others in the light of
the good you do in them, not in relation to the
wrongs I have experienced from them. Free me
from expecting the worst from old associates, so
that I can receive them as the persons you are making new in Christ, in whose name I pray. Amen.

DECEMBER 29

"Welcome Him Back"
Read Philemon verses 15–20

So if you still consider me a comrade-
in-arms, welcome him back as you
would me.

Philemon verse 17

Jesus' intercession for each of us is echoed in this
Pauline intercession for Onesimus. The great act
of intercession in which Jesus restores us to fellowship with God is the model for the healing of
all broken relationships.

Compare verse 20 with verse 7.

PRAYER: Dear Jesus, help me to put to use with
others what I have experienced from you, so that
through my acceptance of them they may begin to
experience your acceptance, through Jesus Christ.
Amen.

DECEMBER 30

"I Know You"
Read Philemon verses 21–22

I know you well enough to know you will.
   You'll probably go far beyond what I've
   written.

Philemon verse 21

We know that, a number of years after this letter
was written, a man by the name of Onesimus was
bishop in Ephesus. Was it the same man? Many
think so. Paul's confidence in Philemon was well
founded. The gospel broke through yet another
barrier created by sin and made a community in
which Christ's love reigned.

   What effect might the request for a guest room
have had on Philemon?

PRAYER: Thank you, Lord, for brothers and sisters
in the faith who do what you command, who
share your love and bring me joy. Grant that, besides benefiting by such a community, I may benefit others. In Jesus Christ. Amen.

DECEMBER 31

"My Coworkers"
Read Philemon verses 23–25

> Epaphras, my cellmate in the cause of
>   Christ, says hello. Also my coworkers
> Mark, Aristarchus, Demas, and Luke.
> > Philemon verses 23–24

Paul never pretended to go it alone. He was immersed in a sea of interdependence. In every part of the world, in every conceivable circumstance, the Holy Spirit provided "co-workers" in the life of faith.

Who are some of your co-workers?

PRAYER: "Refresh Thy people on their toilsome way, Lead us from night to never-ending day; Fill all our lives with love and grace divine, And glory, laud, and praise be ever Thine" (Daniel C. Roberts, "God of Our Fathers, Whose Almighty Hand," *The Hymnbook*, 515). *Amen.*

Topic Index

Scripture Index

7:14 Feb. 27	11:33 April 1
7:18 Feb. 28	12:1 April 2
7:23 March 1	12:2 April 3
7:24 March 2	12:3 April 4
8:1 March 3	12:4 April 5
8:3 March 4	12:6–7 April 6
8:6 March 5	12:11 April 7
8:9 March 6	12:14 April 8
8:11 March 7	13:4 April 9
8:14 March 8	13:7 April 10
8:15–16 March 9	13:9 April 11
8:19 March 10	13:12 April 12
8:22 March 11	14:1 April 13
8:26 March 12	14:6 April 14
8:35 March 14	14:8 April 15
8:38–39 March 15	14:10 April 16
9:3 March 16	14:13 April 17
9:8 March 17	14:15 April 18
9:16 March 18	14:19 April 19
9:21 March 19	14:23 April 20
9:27 March 20	15:1 April 21
9:32 March 21	15:6 April 22
10:3 March 22	15:7 April 23
10:13 March 23	15:15 April 24
10:14 March 24	15:17 April 25
10:21 March 25	15:23 April 26
11:5 March 26	15:26 April 27
11:8 March 27	15:30 April 28
11:12 March 28	16:1–2 April 29
11:16 March 29	16:3 April 30
11:17–18 March 30	16:17 May 1
11:25 March 31	16:27 May 2